D0515702

Aretha Franklin

SINGER

Muhammad Ali

Maya Angelou

Josephine Baker

George Washington Carver

Ray Charles

Johnnie Cochran

Bill Cosby

Frederick Douglass

W.E.B. Du Bois

Jamie Foxx

Aretha Franklin

Marcus Garvey

Savion Glover

Alex Haley

Jimi Hendrix

Gregory Hines

Langston Hughes

Jesse Jackson

Magic Johnson

Scott Joplin

Coretta Scott King

Martin Luther King Jr.

Spike Lee

Malcolm X

Bob Marley

Thurgood Marshall

Barack Obama

Jesse Owens

Rosa Parks

Colin Powell

Condoleezza Rice

Chris Rock

Will Smith

Clarence Thomas

Sojourner Truth

Harriet Tubman

Nat Turner

Madam C.J. Walker

Booker T. Washington

Oprah Winfrey

Stevie Wonder

Tiger Woods

Aretha Franklin

SINGER

Heather Lehr Wagner

CHELSEA HOUSE
PUBLISHERS
An imprint of Infobase Publishing

Aretha Franklin

Copyright © 2010 by Infobase Publishing

Chelsea House
An imprint of Infobase Publishing
132 West 31st Street
New York, NY 10001

Library of Congress Cataloging-in-Publication Data

Wagner, Heather Lehr.
Aretha Franklin : singer / by Heather Lehr Wagner.
    p.   cm. — (Black Americans of achievement. Legacy edition)
 Includes bibliographical references and index.
 ISBN 978-1-60413-712-5 (hardcover)
1. Franklin, Aretha—Juvenile literature. 2. Singers—United States—Biography—Juvenile literature. 3. African American singers—Biography—Juvenile literature. 4. Soul musicians—United States—Biography—Juvenile literature. I. Title. II. Series.
ML3930.F68W34 2010
782.421644092—dc22   [B]   2009050605

Chelsea House books are available at special discounts when purchased in bulk quantities for businesses, associations, institutions, or sales promotions. Please call our Special Sales Department in New York at (212) 967-8800 or (800) 322-8755.

You can find Chelsea House on the World Wide Web at http://www.chelseahouse.com.

Text design by Keith Trego
Cover design by Keith Trego
Composition by Keith Trego
Cover printed by Bang Printing, Brainerd, MN
Book printed and bound by Bang Printing, Brainerd, MN
Date printed: July 2010
Printed in the United States of America

10 9 8 7 6 5 4 3 2 1

This book is printed on acid-free paper.

All links and Web addresses were checked and verified to be correct at the time of publication. Because of the dynamic nature of the Web, some addresses and links may have changed since publication and may no longer be valid.

Contents

In the Spotlight

Early on the chilly morning of January 20, 2009, more than a million people gathered along the National Mall in Washington, D.C., eager to see history being made. The occasion was the inauguration of the forty-fourth president of the United States, Barack Obama, the nation's first African-American president. As the crowds gathered in the vast space between the Washington Monument and the Capitol, many more prepared to watch the inauguration on television or the Internet.

The inauguration began with opening remarks by Senator Dianne Feinstein of California and an invocation, or opening prayer, by minister Rick Warren, founder and senior pastor of the Saddleback Church and author of the popular book *The Purpose Driven Life*. Then, Senator Feinstein returned to the podium to introduce the "world-renowned musical artist Aretha Franklin."

With these words, Aretha Franklin stepped to the front of the stage and picked up a microphone as the crowd cheered. Elegantly dressed in a silver-gray wool coat and matching hat, which sported a large bow with sparkling crystals, Franklin confidently looked out at the vast sea of people. The gleaming Capitol behind her made an impressive backdrop.

The opening notes of Samuel F. Smith's "My Country 'Tis of Thee" swelled up, and Franklin began to sing. The warm, soaring notes of her vocals gave the traditional song a new interpretation and offered a fitting tribute for the new president from the woman dubbed the "Queen of Soul." It was one more milestone for Franklin. Having sung at the pre-inaugural concert for President Jimmy Carter in 1977 and the inaugural ball of President Bill Clinton in 1993, she was now performing during the inauguration ceremony of yet another president.

At the age of 66, Franklin had experienced many milestones in her career. But her performance at President Obama's inauguration would remind those in attendance and others watching on video of how extraordinary a singer she was and what an amazing career she had enjoyed.

While many in the crowd were visibly moved by Franklin's rendition of "My Country 'Tis of Thee," Franklin later told CNN's Larry King that she was displeased with the final result of her performance, blaming the cold weather for negatively impacting her singing. "Mother Nature was not very kind to me," she said the day after the inauguration. "I'm going to deal with her when I get home. It, by no means, was my standard. . . . [But] I was delighted and thrilled to be there. That was the most important thing, not so much the performance, but just to be there and to see this great man go into office— the promise of tomorrow coming to pass."

As always, her influence extended beyond the power of her vocals. For days afterward, attention focused not only on Franklin's performance but also on her fashion choices. The distinctive gray wool hat with its large, crystal-bedecked

Aretha Franklin performs at the inauguration of Barack Obama as the forty-fourth president of the United States on the steps of the Capitol Building in Washington, D.C., on January 20, 2009.

bow was the subject of intense scrutiny. The hat's designer, Luke Song, received more than 5,000 requests for the headgear Franklin had worn. The original, a custom-made design, had cost more than $500. After demand for the hat skyrocketed, Song marketed a less expensive version for $179. The Smithsonian Institution asked Franklin to donate the hat to its exhibit on the inauguration; it would be displayed alongside the inaugural gown worn by First Lady Michelle Obama. Franklin eventually agreed, and following a display at the Smithsonian the hat eventually will be displayed at Barack Obama's presidential library. The hat even earned its own Facebook page, with more than 100,000 fans.

Following the inauguration, Franklin also provided President Obama with several gifts that had deep, personal meaning to her. In interviews, Franklin frequently discusses the importance of her relationship with her father, the prominent Detroit minister C.L. Franklin. At Obama's inauguration, Aretha Franklin presented the president with 17 sermons by her late father, as well as a Bible. She gave Michelle Obama a gold brooch studded with diamonds and presented Obama's two daughters with a collection of gospel/Christian hip-hop music. "My dad's sermons, I thought, would be an excellent gift for the president as he's a fairly young man," Franklin told National Public Radio on March 17, 2009, for the program *Tell Me More.* "They definitely hold a lot of wisdom that I thought would be beneficial for the president."

ANOTHER MILESTONE

Franklin's performance at the inauguration of President Obama was yet another highlight in a career that has spanned more than five decades. *Rolling Stone* describes her as "one of the most influential and important voices in the history of popular music." Her recordings have spanned several different genres of music, including gospel, rhythm and blues (R&B), American standards, pop, and soul. In 1987, she became the first female recording artist inducted into the Rock and Roll Hall of Fame. In addition to her soaring vocal skills, she is also an accomplished pianist and songwriter. In fact, several of Franklin's most successful recordings are of songs she wrote herself.

Franklin began performing as a teenager, accompanying her father on tours of the gospel circuit. Signed to a recording contract when she was barely 20, Franklin released several interpretations of slow ballads and standards. It was not until 1967, however, that she found commercial success recording the distinctive songs that would dramatically influence pop music and showcase her unique style. Following the success of popular singles such as "Respect," "Think," and "Chain of Fools," Franklin earned the nickname "Lady Soul." Soon, she would be known as the "Queen of Soul."

During her career, Franklin has made more than a dozen million-selling singles (in fact, more million-sellers than any woman in recording history) and recorded 20 number-one R&B hits. She is cited as a major influence of countless female recording artists, from Mary J. Blige to Mariah Carey to Jennifer Hudson.

Though astonishing triumphs have marked Franklin's career, family tragedies and career setbacks have haunted many of her

IN HER OWN WORDS...

In her 1999 autobiography, *Aretha: From These Roots*, Franklin described the energy and enthusiasm for music that continues to inspire her to record and perform:

> I have dreams for the future. . . . God has been so good to me; my life has been and is rewarding, exciting, and creative. And surely the best is yet to come. There are many songs that I want to sing. And sing . . .

greatest accomplishments. Difficulties have beset her from an early age: Her parents separated when Franklin was six years old, and her mother died four years later. Franklin was a single mother of two boys before she was 17 years old. And later, her father was shot by burglars in his home and died of the injuries he sustained during the attack.

Despite these challenges and changing tastes in popular music, Franklin has remained a force in the recording industry. Throughout her career, she has known and collaborated with many of music's greatest stars. Her life story is an inspiring account of the evolution of popular music, of a woman determined to shape her career on her terms, and of a child prodigy whose voice continues to thrill and amaze audiences well into her seventh decade.

2

Childhood in Detroit

Aretha Louise Franklin was born on March 25, 1942, in Memphis, Tennessee. The fourth of five children born to Clarence LaVaughn Franklin and Barbara Siggers Franklin, she entered a family in which music played an important role long before she first began to sing.

Her father, known as C.L. Franklin, was a dynamic Baptist minister who grew up in a rural Mississippi marked by racism, religious prejudice, and violence against minorities, particularly black Americans. Jim Crow laws—a system of local and state laws in the United States enacted between 1876 and 1965 that segregated the black and white races in all public places—existed throughout the South. The church was one of the few safe havens, and African-American churches provided the center of social life for many in the community.

C.L. Franklin's biological father, Willie Walker, was drafted to serve in the U.S. Army during World War I. After returning from war, Walker abandoned his family. C.L. was about four years old. He later took the last name of his stepfather, a farmer named Henry Franklin, whom his mother married when he was about five.

The family survived by sharecropping—renting a plot of land, farming it, and paying rent with a share of the crops the land produced. The main crop was cotton. As a teenager, C.L. Franklin was expected to help his family farm the land. But increasingly, C.L. felt called to become a preacher and, at the age of 18, he became the pastor of a small church in Mississippi. As his reputation grew, he became a circuit preacher, traveling between four small churches in rural communities. At 19, C.L. Franklin married his first wife, Alene Gaines. Little is known of the marriage or how long it lasted, but at some point after his first marriage ended, C.L. met Barbara Siggers at a church in Shelby, Mississippi.

The fourth of seven children, Barbara Siggers spent much of her youth in Memphis, where she was exposed to the growing presence of gospel music in African-American churches. By the time her family moved to more rural Shelby, Barbara was in her late teens and had developed a lovely singing voice. It was her singing voice that first impressed C.L. when he met her. The couple shared a passion for music and a dream of leaving rural Mississippi to build a better life for themselves. On June 3, 1936, they married, and C.L. adopted Barbara's young son, Vaughn. Soon after, C.L. became the pastor of the small New Salem Baptist Church in Memphis, where the family relocated.

FROM MEMPHIS TO DETROIT

By the time Aretha Louise Franklin was born in 1942, the family had grown to include two more children—a daughter, Erma, and a son, Cecil. Aretha was named for her father's two sisters. C.L. Franklin had come to Memphis's New Salem Baptist Church as a country preacher, but he developed a

The Reverend C.L. Franklin, Aretha Franklin's father, poses for a portrait circa 1965. An enormously popular preacher, C.L. Franklin would have a recording career of his own because of his influential sermons on the gospel circuit.

more sophisticated speaking style in Memphis. In *Singing in a Strange Land*, a biography of C.L. Franklin, Nick Salvatore writes that C.L.'s clothes, when he first arrived as preacher, were unfashionable and worn, but he was a compelling speaker and had overwhelming charisma, even as a 24-year-old. In addition, his humble country beginnings influenced many in the congregation who nurtured their own dreams of bettering themselves—of moving to a new place and seeking a different life for themselves and their families.

It was at New Salem that C.L. Franklin began to perfect his unique speaking style. He delivered sermons in a distinctive manner that emphasized the idea of the pastor's message being a performance, rather than simply a speech to be read aloud. In this call-and-response style, the preacher would invite members of the congregation to respond out loud to what he was saying. According to *Singing in a Strange Land*, Franklin became such a popular preacher that his church attracted people from all over Memphis. The church had seating for 400 people, but on most Sundays the church was full and people stood in the aisles and in the back to listen.

Shortly after Aretha's birth, the family moved to Buffalo, New York, where C.L. had been invited to lead the Friendship Baptist Church while Barbara served as choir director and pianist. C.L. created a weekly radio program in Buffalo in which his sermons were broadcast on a local radio station. His sermons often reflected his thoughts on what the end of World War II would mean for race relations in the United States, as well as on the idea of social equality. In 1945, the year the war ended, C.L. was invited to speak at the National Baptist Convention in Detroit, Michigan. It would prove a pivotal moment in his career. His speaking style was so impressive in that large setting at Olympia Stadium that he was invited to become the pastor of New Bethel Baptist Church in Detroit. The family moved there when Aretha was about three years old.

A THRIVING COMMUNITY

When the Franklin family arrived in Detroit in 1946, an active African-American community was growing on the city's west side. Many black families had chosen to leave the challenging life of sharecropping they had known in the South and migrate to northern states such as Michigan in search of greater opportunities during the postwar period.

In Detroit, C.L. Franklin quickly became a prominent member of the community. His sermons were recorded and broadcast not only in the city but also on radio stations throughout much of the country. Civil rights activist Jesse Jackson remembered listening to C.L. Franklin every Sunday night on a radio broadcast in his home in South Carolina. In an interview in June 2003 for the Detroit African American History Project, hosted by Wayne State University, Jackson stated:

> Before we had television, really before we had cable and all of this, radio and records were the great mediums and Reverend C.L. Franklin's albums were a great source of inspiration. . . . In many ways the first real kind of a superstar, if I may use that kind of language, of Black preaching was Reverend C.L. Franklin. He was by far the most imitated Black preacher. The most emulated. The one looked up to the most.

Jackson recalled listening to many of the great gospel artists who were affiliated with New Bethel Baptist Church. He would later become a friend of the Franklin family and even stay at their home when he was visiting Detroit.

As C.L. Franklin's reputation as a preacher was growing, however, his marriage was falling apart. When Aretha was six years old, her parents agreed to separate. Her mother, Barbara, moved back to Buffalo with Aretha's half brother, Vaughn. Barbara's parents and other family members had moved to Buffalo, and so she lived with her parents and worked as a nurse's aide. Aretha and the other children remained with their father. In her autobiography, *Aretha: From These Roots*, she suggests that the decision of who the children would live with was made principally for financial reasons:

> Mom couldn't afford to raise five children on a nurse's aide's salary. However, she communicated with us by phone and regular visits. She never lost sight of her children or her parenting responsibilities—and her visits continued regularly. She sent us beautiful gifts, and we traveled to Buffalo to spend the summers with her yearly.

Aretha later recalled enjoying those annual visits to her mother's home in Cold Springs, a middle-class African-American neighborhood with wide, tree-lined streets. There was a piano in the back room, and the home was often full of relatives. But the house had only two bedrooms, which were already occupied by Aretha's grandparents, mother, and half brother. So during those annual visits, Aretha and her brother and sisters stayed with a next-door neighbor, who taught Aretha to crochet—a hobby she still enjoys.

While Aretha's mother worked at Buffalo General Hospital, Aretha and her brother and sisters would ride their bikes through the neighborhood or swim in a public pool. Music was an important part of life in both parents' homes, and Aretha's mother was known for her soaring gospel voice. At some point the idea of Aretha staying with her mother may have been considered, since she notes in her autobiography that she attended a public school in Buffalo for a short time. But eventually Aretha returned to Detroit, to its music and the dynamic climate of New Bethel Baptist Church, which would heavily influence her own musical talent and style.

LIFE AT NEW BETHEL

C.L. Franklin and his children lived in the parish house of the church, a six-bedroom home on Boston Boulevard. The neighborhood was noted for its carefully landscaped lawns. The backyard of the Franklin home boasted several fruit trees, including pear, plum, and apple trees, and offered beautiful flowers in the spring and fruit in the summer.

In the Franklin home, music played a significant role in family entertainment. The house had two pianos, including a grand piano in the living room. Both Aretha and her sisters, Erma and Carolyn, took piano lessons from a piano teacher who came to their home to teach them. Despite the lessons, Aretha never learned to sight-read music; instead she learned to play by ear. Her ability to mimic the songs she heard on the radio by playing them on the piano was the first clue to her father of her talent.

Growing up, Aretha heard many prominent musicians playing in the living room of the Franklin home. The great jazz pianist Art Tatum was C.L.'s friend. Nat King Cole played and sang when he visited. Gospel musician James Cleveland taught Aretha some basic piano chords. When musicians were not performing live in the Franklin home, records and the radio ensured that jazz, blues, and gospel were a constant in the background. Occasionally, after Aretha had gone to bed, her father would wake her and ask her to play the piano and

DID YOU KNOW?

Aretha Franklin spent only a brief time studying piano when she was a girl. She did not enjoy the piano lessons her father had arranged for his three daughters. Instead, she began teaching herself to play by listening to popular songs and the pianists who played at the Franklin home. She then mimicked them, copying their style and slowly working out, note by note, how to play the songs. She became such an accomplished pianist that she often played in her studio recordings, especially during her early work with Atlantic Records. In recent years, she has returned to the piano, taking lessons in classical piano at the prestigious Juilliard School in order to perfect her skill.

sing for those who had gathered at the home. In addition, she also studied music in school; in third grade, Aretha joined the glee club, where she learned about harmony. She also joined the school band but was too late to get the instrument she wanted: the flute. Instead she was given the tuba—the only instrument left!

C.L.'s parents lived with the family when Aretha was young. His mother, who Aretha referred to as Big Mama, ran the household and handled punishing the children when they did something wrong. His father, known as Big Papa, had suffered a stroke that affected his speech and movement, so he spent most of his time in an upstairs bedroom. In order to help with the chores, C.L. hired housekeepers to do the housework and cooking. Aretha studied the cooking techniques of these women and Big Mama, learning to make Southern specialties such as ham hocks, fried corn, and pineapple upside-down cake.

Because C.L.'s powerful preaching drew large crowds to New Bethel Baptist Church, the congregation grew to 4,500 and a new building was needed. The new church was an impressive structure of light-colored brick with stained-glass windows. It was located on Hastings Street, one of the centers of African-American life in Detroit in the 1940s and 1950s. At the time, Hastings Street was one of the few areas in the city where blacks could own and operate businesses, including bars and music clubs. The street was not only an economic backbone for the community, it was also its entertainment center; on any given night, jazz and blues music could be heard drifting out from many of the clubs that lined the street.

Now ensconced in a new church, C.L. developed his style to match his growing fame and prominence in the community. In her autobiography, Aretha described her father as "a handsome man who stood over six feet tall. . . . He took great pride in his appearance and never dressed in drab colors. He was style and class at its best."

Aretha Franklin's Sisters

The Franklin home was filled with music and talent. While Aretha went on to superstar status, her two sisters, Erma and Carolyn, were also talented singers, composers, and performers in their own right.

It was older sister Erma who first began the family tradition of singing with the church choir, performing at the age of five when the family was still living in Buffalo. Berry Gordy, who later founded the Motown record label, selected Erma as the most talented of the Franklin sisters. In the early days of his career, he attempted to get funding for several recordings featuring Erma, but the funding could not be raised. She attended college instead.

Erma later went with Aretha and her father to New York, where C.L. sought to obtain recording contracts for both daughters. Eventually, Capitol Records signed Aretha and Epic Records signed Erma. When Erma's solo career failed to take off, she worked instead as a vocalist for a big band orchestra. In 1967, Erma recorded "Piece of My Heart." The song earned her a Grammy nomination the following year, but her record company dissolved before releasing a planned album. The song was later recorded by Janis Joplin and became Joplin's signature number.

Erma subsequently worked as a computer programmer and then, with sister Carolyn, joined Aretha as one of her backup singers. Both sisters sang on Aretha's hit "Respect," and in fact some sources have suggested that Erma designed the famous "Sock it to me" refrain in that song. In later life, Erma worked for nearly 30 years for Boysville of Michigan, a charity that dealt with troubled children. She died of cancer in 2002.

Younger sister Carolyn was yet another Franklin woman with extraordinary talent. Born in Memphis in 1945, she too gained experience performing gospel music while singing with the New Bethel Baptist Choir. She sang background on several of Aretha's numbers before being signed by RCA as a solo artist. But because RCA was not known for producing soul music, Carolyn did not have the kind of supportive producers Aretha enjoyed at Atlantic. Carolyn had several minor hits for the label, including "It's True I'm Gonna Miss You," which reached number 23 on the R&B charts in 1969.

In addition to working as a backup singer for her older sister, Carolyn wrote several songs that Aretha recorded, including "Angel" and "Ain't No Way," both of which became million-sellers. She died of cancer in 1988 at the age of 43. Shortly before her death, she achieved her dream of graduating from college.

As a young girl, Aretha sang with New Bethel Baptist's junior choir. When she was about nine or ten years old, she sang her first solo in church. She stood behind the pianist and gazed out at the congregation, where some 1,500 people were seated, waiting to hear her perform. Then she saw the smiling face of Big Mama, nodding and offering silent encouragement. Aretha began to sing the opening phrases of "Jesus Be a Fence Around Me," a gospel tune recently recorded by Sam Cooke. After the success of her first solo performance, Aretha routinely sang in her father's church, both as a soloist and as part of a gospel quartet directed by James Cleveland, who would later become a noted gospel artist. Aretha recalled that her grandmother was a constant source of visible and vocal support, often calling, "Sing out, Aretha!" as she performed.

Big Mama also called out her support and approval as her son preached. As previously mentioned, C.L. welcomed and encouraged his congregation to participate, to respond vocally to what he was saying. If the church was too quiet, he might stop in the middle of preaching to instruct a member of the congregation to poke a neighbor and wake them up. After the sermon, C.L. himself would occasionally sing, performing such hymns as "Father, I Stretch My Hands to Thee" or "Old Ship of Zion." Aretha believed that her father could have become a successful vocalist had he chosen to concentrate only on singing. Between C.L.'s powerful preaching and the singing of numerous spirituals, the church services were emotional events that often lasted several hours.

CLARA WARD

Music fans have described the 1950s as "the golden age of gospel." Many of the musical artists most identified with gospel music during that decade traveled to Detroit. Many performed at New Bethel Baptist. But no gospel singer was more influential on Aretha Franklin than Clara Ward, who has been called one of the greatest soloists in gospel history.

Gospel singer Clara Ward poses for a portrait circa 1955 in New York City. A friend of Franklin's father, Ward would have a significant influence on Aretha Franklin's musical development.

Born in Philadelphia in 1924, Clara Ward traveled the country with her group, the Ward Singers, which also featured Marion Williams, who would herself become an international gospel star. Ward was credited with focusing on the entertainment end of performing gospel music. She took the sound from the church to other performing venues, even Las Vegas, and brought flair and glamour to gospel music. At a time when most gospel groups performed in long robes (either black or white), the Ward Singers performed in sequined gowns and wore elaborate hairdos.

As a girl, Aretha recalled being deeply impressed, not only by Clara Ward's extraordinary voice, but also by her ladylike manner when eating fried chicken. She would later try to imitate both her performing style and her manners. Franklin noted in her autobiography, "The style of gospel singing exemplified by Clara Ward became the great musical influence of my early childhood."

Just as Aretha was developing musically, tragedy struck. When Aretha was 10 years old, her mother died suddenly of a heart attack. C.L. gathered the children together in the kitchen to tell them the sad news. "I cannot describe the pain, nor will I try," Aretha later recalled in *Aretha: From These Roots*. "Pain is sometimes a private matter, and the pain of small children losing their mother defies description."

The family traveled to Buffalo for the funeral. After the service, Aretha spent a long time sitting on the sidewalk, across from her mother's home, thinking of her mother and remembering the time they had spent together.

3

Preacher's Daughter

Even with her mother's death, Aretha Franklin recalls memories of an idyllic childhood in Detroit in the 1950s—a city where children could safely walk wherever they wanted or catch the bus or streetcar for 10 cents a ride. Aretha's father often sent her on errands for him—to carry messages to people in the neighborhood, to do the shopping at the drugstore or grocery store, or to pick up soul food or hot dogs from a local restaurant.

Detroit at the time was also a hotbed of musical talent. Many singers who would go on to become major recording superstars grew up with Aretha in Detroit. One of her childhood friends was future singer, songwriter, and producer Smokey Robinson, who would have his first hit at the age of 18 with his group, the Miracles. At the time, however, he was simply Aretha's brother Cecil's closest friend. Others in the neighborhood who would go on to fame were Diana Ross,

Jackie Wilson, and four young men who would gain fame as the Four Tops: Levi Stubbs, Abdul "Duke" Fakir, Renaldo "Obie" Benson, and Lawrence Payton.

James Cleveland, who would become a prominent gospel star and a minister, contributed to the development of Aretha's early sound. Cleveland was still a young man in his early twenties when he began serving as director of music at the New Bethel Baptist Church. He had already written several gospel songs, many of which became standards, including "Grace Is Sufficient" and "Peace Be Still." His music relied on elaborate harmonies and rich chords. He reorganized New Bethel's music program, highlighting Aretha and many of the other talented singers who formed part of the congregation. Sam Cooke, who would gain fame as a recording artist with such songs as "You Send Me," performed at New Bethel as a teenager as a member of a gospel group called the Soul Stirrers.

James Cleveland

As choir director of New Bethel, James Cleveland was enormously influential on Aretha Franklin's singing. Cleveland would go on to a rich and varied musical career of his own, becoming known as the "Crown Prince of Gospel."

Cleveland was born in 1931 in Chicago, Illinois, where he attended the Pilgrim Baptist Church. He first began singing gospel music as part of a choir directed by Thomas A. Dorsey, one of the early pioneers of the gospel sound, and performed his first solo with the choir when he was just eight years old. Although his family could not afford a piano, Cleveland managed to teach himself the instrument by studying the pianists at church and then practicing the finger movements on the windowsill or on imaginary keys.

Cleveland began composing gospel music as a teenager and performed it with the Thorn Gospel Crusaders, a group formed by singers in Cleveland's neighborhood. In 1948, his song "Grace Is Sufficient" was published. By 1950, he was recording gospel numbers under the Apollo label. As his musical career developed, he founded several gospel groups. The earliest

At the same time, C.L. Franklin was becoming a nationally prominent figure. As previously noted, his radio show brought his message to distant listeners, and many of his sermons were recorded on albums and internationally distributed. Because of his popularity, he was given a contract with Chess Records, a recording label known primarily for its blues artists, such as Muddy Waters, and its R&B artists, including Chuck Berry and Bo Diddley. Chess would eventually release more than 60 of C.L.'s albums.

Churches around the country asked C.L. to come and speak to their congregation. He was now known as "the man with the million-dollar voice." Soon, he was accompanying touring gospel artists such as Clara Ward and the Dixie Hummingbirds. The gospel groups would sing, and then the program would end with one of C.L.'s sermons. Eventually, C.L. decided to organize his own traveling revival show, in which he would deliver

was the Gospel Chimes, which became famous for performing and recording numbers Cleveland had composed and arranged.

Cleveland came to New Bethel Baptist Church in the 1950s to serve as choir director and minister of music. He later signed with Savoy Records and recorded more than 60 albums for the label, one of which—*Peace Be Still*—was so successful that it held a spot on the gospel charts for more than 15 years and sold more than a million copies. In the 1960s, Cleveland became a minister and moved to Los Angeles, California, where he served as pastor at New Greater Harvest Baptist Church and then at Cornerstone Institutional Baptist Church. He believed that gospel music and preaching were deeply connected, with both serving to provide teaching and worship.

While Aretha and others he had mentored eventually became pop music stars, Cleveland remained committed to gospel music, composing, arranging, and performing in the genre for many decades. He died of heart failure in 1991.

powerful sermons while accompanied by a choir and gospel singers, such as Clara Ward. Because the tours would take him away from home for long stretches of time, Aretha and her siblings were cared for by their grandmother, Big Mama.

As a teenager, Aretha enjoyed many of the fads that were popular in Detroit in the 1950s. At first, this meant roller-skating at the Arcadia. Aretha and her friends spent most weekends and some weekdays traveling by trolley to the Arcadia roller rink, where they would skate to popular music and meet boys. Her youthful infatuations would eventually lead to a very adult situation: When she was only 14 years old, Aretha discovered that she was pregnant. C.L. Franklin stood by his daughter, and her family helped support her during this difficult time. She dropped out of school and gave birth to a son, Clarence.

After Clarence was born, C.L. was increasingly concerned about the need to spend more time with Aretha. But the demands of his work at New Bethel Baptist and the growing requests for him to speak around the country made it difficult. Finally, he came up with the perfect solution: Aretha would travel with him and perform as part of his gospel revue.

ON THE ROAD

Traveling with her father opened Aretha's eyes to what life was like beyond the relatively sheltered and privileged life she had enjoyed in Detroit. Because many restaurants and hotels were segregated in those days, they would often have to drive for several hours before finding a restaurant that would serve them or a hotel that would give them a place to stay. (In fact, segregation was one reason why so many prominent musicians and artists had gravitated to the Franklin home. When they came to Detroit, they knew that C.L. would always welcome them with a meal and an offer to stay the night.) In her autobiography, Aretha remembered the experience of traveling with her father as a special time. Because of the difficulty of finding a restaurant that would serve them, they would often stop at small grocery stores and buy cheese, crackers, and soda to eat on the road.

Aretha's grandmother had agreed to watch her infant son while she traveled and performed. Her father paid Aretha $50 for each performance. It was an extraordinary opportunity for the teenaged Aretha to perform before so many audiences, to study what went into making a successful evening's performance, and to see how her father and the other gospel singers interacted with the congregations.

At each city, the revue included a full church service as well as music. In addition to Aretha, there were two female singers: Sammy Bryant and Lucy Branch. They sang first, and then Aretha would perform just before C.L.'s sermon. Largely self-taught on the piano, Aretha would accompany herself. In those early years, her performing relied on mimicking the styles of artists she knew in Detroit. Her piano playing reflected the dramatic chords and flourishes of her choir director, James Cleveland, and as a singer she often copied the vocal style of Sam Cooke or other singers she knew. Eventually, her father urged her not to imitate other people but to develop her own style.

Her father's preaching provided the dramatic conclusion to the evening. Aretha was often moved by the sight of so many people, in so many different cities, responding to her father's message. His sermons focused on many different topics, including discussions of civil rights and race relations—two issues that were particularly important at a time when the civil rights movement was just beginning to take shape. Messages such as "The Eagle Stirreth Her Nest" became classics and added to C.L.'s fame.

HER FIRST ALBUM

Although Aretha was now a mother and had spent time as part of a national gospel tour as a performing artist, she was also still just a teenager. Back in Detroit, she and her friends continued to spend time at the Arcadia roller-skating rink. She soon fell in love with a young man and again became pregnant.

Aretha was forced to deliver the devastating news to her father that she was pregnant for the second time. Her father again was supportive, but he told her that she needed to become a responsible adult now and take steps to provide for her children. At the age of 17, she gave birth to her second child, a boy she named Eddie.

Thanks to the success of the tours and his records, C.L. was able to move his family to a larger home in a prosperous section of Detroit. Aretha remembered it in her autobiography as "the most beautiful home I had ever seen." It was made of white brick and sat on a half acre of land. The home boasted a built-in refrigerator with silver handles; distinctive tile and woodwork; and a special study for C.L., as well as a separate apartment for Aretha's brother, Cecil.

Aretha was not the only member of the family with an interest in performing. Her sisters, Erma and Carolyn, were also interested in musical careers. In the 1960s, Erma participated in a musical tour with Lloyd Price, an R&B singer. Both Cecil and Erma attended college in Atlanta, where Erma sang in several local clubs. After graduating from high school, Carolyn became a composer, writing several songs that Aretha would later record.

In 1956, Chess Records, the label that had successfully recorded and released several of C.L. Franklin's albums, approached him and expressed their interest in producing an album featuring Aretha. C.L. agreed. *The Gospel Sound of Aretha Franklin* was released later that year. Many of the gospel songs featured on this debut album had been recorded at New Bethel when Aretha was 14 years old; others were recorded during services on the road. All were recorded live.

The album features the gospel sound that Aretha had learned at her home church and had perfected on the road.

Franklin sings into a microphone during her first recording session at Columbia Records in New York City, in 1961. Although Franklin would later become the first woman inducted into the Rock and Roll Hall of Fame, she struggled in her early career to make a name for herself, despite her immense talent.

The nine songs she recorded reflect all of Aretha's early major influences. Three of the songs—"There Is a Fountain Filled with Blood," "The Day Is Past and Gone," and "While the Blood Runs Warm"—are those that Clara Ward often performed. Others, including "He Will Wash You Whiter Than Snow" and "Jesus Be a Fence Around Me," were the first two solos Aretha performed with the young adult choir at her church. It also includes some of Aretha's favorite gospel songs, such as "I Am Sealed" and "Precious Lord." The album exposed Aretha's voice to a new audience. It would be reissued 30 years later under the title *Aretha Gospel*.

BACK ON THE ROAD

While Big Mama cared for Aretha's two young sons, Aretha went back on the road with her father. Los Angeles was one of her favorite destinations, a trip she and her father made by car. It took three and a half days and three nights of driving to reach California. Once there, they would stay at the Watkins Hotel, one of the Los Angeles hotels that welcomed African-American guests. It was also a place where they might see Nat Cole or Sam Cooke.

Aretha was impressed that so many of the young men she knew who had started out performing gospel music at New Bethel had become so-called "crossover" artists, successfully making the transition from gospel to R&B and other forms of

IN HER OWN WORDS...

In an interview with the *Washington Post* in 2008, Aretha Franklin reflected on her decision not to sign with the then start-up label Motown:

Many of my friends were there at Motown. The studio was only a few blocks from where my dad's home was, where we lived. So I would just go over to the studio to see who was recording, just to say hello, maybe to Smokey [Robinson] or Mary Wells, or someone who I was friends with. But I'm glad that my career took the path it did. As I understood it they had to get special permission to be paid. I'm not really sure what it was, but in my instance, coming up, I was able to handle my own money and I didn't have to ask anyone for anything. And those artists, I believe, did. They had to go through a process to get a check written. Certainly Motown presented their artists in a first class way. They did have some of the things that the other labels didn't have, which were the grooming schools where they had to sit and take different classes in knowing how to speak to the press and so on. So they had some very good things on their label that other labels didn't have. But then other labels had further reaching distribution, internationally, than Motown did. There was a different respect to begin with, in the industry, between a Columbia Records and Motown. Later on, Motown became the industry giant that it did.

popular music. In her autobiography, Aretha notes that there were close ties between many of the artists who specialized in gospel and pop music at that time. Even in those days, she and her father were looking ahead to a time when her career might move in the direction of pop music.

Although her father was her chief adviser and both of them were committed to the idea of her pursuing a pop music career, Aretha made her own decisions in certain areas. In 1960, a group of agents in Detroit approached C.L. about representing his daughter. C.L. liked the agents and urged Aretha to sign the contract, but she refused. Soon after, representatives of a Detroit-based record label, Motown, approached Aretha. At the time, Motown was a small label founded by some of the Franklins' friends in Detroit, and C.L. and Aretha felt that they wanted a bigger label to guarantee her both national and international exposure. They refused to sign with Motown, little realizing that it would go on to become one of the most successful and instantly recognizable record labels of all time.

Finally, C.L. took Aretha to New York to meet with Phil Moore, a respected choreographer and musical arranger who had worked with talented African-American performers such as Dorothy Dandridge and Lena Horne. Aretha had expanded her repertoire to include a few popular songs recorded by Sam Cooke, such as "Navajo Trail" and "Ac-Cent-Tchu-Ate the Positive," and she sang these for Moore at their meeting.

In her autobiography, Aretha recalled that Moore's review was positive. "Reverend," he said, "your daughter doesn't need big choreography. She doesn't need to be fluffed up or polished over with New York sophistication. I wouldn't touch or tamper with what she has naturally. She has a very special gift. Just let her do her thing and she'll be fine."

RECORDING A DEMO
The next step in Aretha's career involved recording a demo. The demo is a kind of sample album, designed to showcase

artists' talent and demonstrate to the record companies the range of their voices and their commercial possibilities. For her demo, Aretha sang with a trio of musicians. She focused on "standards," a popular style of music at the time. These were songs, many originating in the big-band era of music of the 1930s and 1940s, that became known as standards because they continued to be performed and recorded many years after their original release date. Some singers who specialized in singing standards include Frank Sinatra, Bing Crosby, Billie Holiday, and Ella Fitzgerald.

Since many African-American female singers, such as Holiday and Fitzgerald, were known for singing standards, C.L. and Aretha decided that this would be a logical starting point for Aretha's transition from gospel to pop music. One of the popular standards she performed on the demo was "My Funny Valentine," written by Richard Rodgers and Lorenz Hart for their 1937 musical, *Babes in Arms*.

C.L. helped Aretha hire her first manager, a woman named Jo King, who took the demo to John Hammond, a successful producer, writer, and music critic who worked at Columbia Records. A white man, Hammond served on the board of the National Association for the Advancement of Colored People (NAACP) and was a major force in helping to integrate the music business. Initially he specialized in jazz and worked with musicians such as Count Basie, Bessie Smith, and Benny Goodman. In the 1940s and 1950s, he spent a large amount of time in Europe, focusing more on classical music. But in the late 1950s, he returned to the United States and began to work for Columbia Records. (Later, Hammond would discover such noteworthy musicians as Bob Dylan and Bruce Springsteen.)

The discovery of Aretha Franklin was a major turning point in Hammond's career. He would describe her as "the greatest singer since Billie Holliday." Hammond decided to market Aretha as a jazz singer, and her first album is full of music highlighting jazz-blues influences. Hammond arranged

In August 1961, Aretha Franklin and John Hammond work together in the recording studio for the first time. Discovering Franklin would be a major turning point in Hammond's career, although his protégé's own career was still years away from superstardom.

for the backup musicians to be skilled jazz performers, and Aretha's first Columbia album features Ray Bryant on piano, Osie Johnson on drums, Skeeter Best and Lord Westbrook on guitars, Milt Hinton and Bill Lee (father of filmmaker Spike Lee) on bass, and Tyree Glenn on trombone. On two of the songs—"Maybe I'm a Fool" and "Right Now"—Aretha plays the piano as well as sings.

These first recording sessions were not designed with the idea of creating an overall concept for an album. Instead, each song she recorded was designed to be sold as a single, to be played on radio or on the jukebox. John Hammond served as producer on all of them. (Ultimately, an album containing all of these singles was released in 1973 under the title *The Great Aretha Franklin*. It even includes a recording of Aretha singing "Over the Rainbow," a song made famous by Judy Garland in the 1939 film *The Wizard of Oz*.)

Attention was given to marketing Aretha as a representative of a new generation of jazz and blues singers. She was given classes in dance and choreography. She was also given lessons in how to conduct herself, how to move on stage. She even had a vocal coach for a brief period. Aretha rehearsed and performed in small clubs and other venues. While she was recording and studying, Aretha was living in New York City, but not alone. C.L. had arranged for a chaperone—a friend of his named Sue Dodds Banks, who had a keen fashion sense. She helped Aretha develop a sense of style and select the right wardrobe for appearances.

In her first days in New York, Aretha lived at the YWCA before finding a place at the Bryant Hotel on Fifty-fourth Street and Broadway. She then lived briefly at the Chelsea Hotel. At the time, Aretha was only 18 years old and her father was still managing her money. At one point he somehow neglected to pay her weekly rent, and she was locked out of her room with her belongings held until the weekly bill was paid. After that embarrassing episode, Aretha left the Chelsea Hotel and moved to a small room in Greenwich Village.

Aretha was busy with her career but found some time to date, mainly other musicians. Although she was getting exposure and singing in clubs, she still had not had a breakout hit. After her expenses were paid, she had little money left over, but she managed to scrimp and save enough to attend concerts featuring some of her old friends, including the Four Tops and Sam Cooke. These acts were playing at the famous Apollo Theater in Harlem, but lacking a number-one hit, Aretha was not invited to perform at the Apollo. Instead, her shows took place in small jazz clubs around New York. She also played on the road, in cities such as Chicago, Illinois, and

Atlanta, Georgia, but always in small venues. She was often the opening act for better-known jazz artists such as John Coltrane and Charlie Mingus or for comedians such as Buddy Hackett and Dick Gregory.

Aretha had made the transition from the gospel circuit to the jazz circuit. But fame and success were still far away.

4

Jazz Singer

In 1961, the International Jazz Critics Poll named Aretha Franklin the New Female Vocal Star. Soon she was receiving greater attention from jazz audiences, and her performances were successful.

Although she was living in New York, she returned home often to see her sons and spend time with her family. Having achieved some success, the 19-year-old Franklin felt that she was well on her way to being a star. Household chores and helping at home were beneath her. "Daddy swiftly brought me back down to earth," Aretha wrote in *From These Roots*, "by telling me to introduce myself to the sink full of dirty dishes. When I finished that, I could mop the kitchen floor." Her father wanted to make sure that she did not allow her early success to make her conceited or arrogant.

As the civil rights movement gained steam across America in the early 1960s, C.L. Franklin, a longtime supporter of racial equality, became involved. He had befriended one of the leaders of the movement, Dr. Martin Luther King Jr., and in 1963 helped King organize an important protest march through the streets of Detroit.

Meanwhile, Franklin continued to record albums for Columbia, although she was no longer working with John Hammond. She had signed a six-year contract with the label, but the executives at Columbia seemed uncertain about how best to capitalize on Aretha's extraordinary vocal talents. Therefore, she alternatively recorded songs for adults and songs for teens.

Franklin was booked to appear on *The Ed Sullivan Show,* a popular television variety program that ran on CBS from 1948 to 1971 and was considered to be an important showcase for actors and musicians. She was scheduled to sing two standards, "Moon River" and "Skylark." She stepped onto the stage, dressed in a silk gown with orange-gold beading, when suddenly a voice sounded over the loudspeakers: "Did Miss Franklin bring another gown?" The censors at the network felt that her dress was too low-cut. Aretha disagreed, but luckily she had brought other gowns with her. She quickly returned to the dressing room to change and wait for the call summoning her back onto the stage.

She waited and waited, but the call did not come. The show had overbooked, and there was not enough time for Franklin to appear and sing. She had been cut from the show.

NEW DIRECTIONS
On a trip back to Detroit, Franklin was introduced to Ted White. Ted was 11 years older than her and had a reputation for dating several women at once. He asked Franklin out, and she accepted—to her father's dismay. C.L. did not like White, worried about his reputation, and was concerned that a relationship with White might distract his daughter from her career.

Aretha Franklin poses for a portrait with her husband and manager
Ted White, circa 1961. Although her father did not like White, Aretha
discovered that her husband's influence led her toward a more contemporary style of music.

White took Franklin to many of the late-night clubs then popular in Detroit. He introduced her to popular acts such as the Temptations. Before long, he had persuaded her to make him her manager. Under White's direction, she began performing with a new backup band, made up principally of Detroit musicians White knew. Even though he was managing and dating Franklin, he continued to see other women as well.

Despite the evidence that White was two-timing her, Aretha had fallen in love with her new manager. In late 1961, White proposed and she accepted. The wedding took place as she toured in Ohio. A justice of the peace married the couple. It must have been yet another disappointment to C.L. Franklin that he was not invited to his daughter's wedding, and that it was not held at New Bethel Baptist.

After their marriage, White established an office in Detroit and signed a few songwriters as clients. In 1964, he and Franklin had a son, Ted White Jr., whom they called Teddy. At the same time, Franklin continued to record and release albums for Columbia, but her hopes for a hugely successful career had not yet materialized. Her albums featured mostly standards that were recorded with large backup bands. Songs such as "How Deep Is the Ocean" and "What a Diff'rence a Day Makes" showcase a popular sound of the time, but they are quite different from the powerful soul sound that would later make Aretha Franklin famous.

In 1963, Franklin was devastated when Dinah Washington, a singer who had been one of her idols, died of an accidental overdose. She was asked to record a tribute album, featuring 10 songs that Washington had made famous. The album, titled *Unforgettable* and released in 1964, would prove to be one of Franklin's most artistically successful efforts for Columbia. But the question remains: Why was someone as immensely talented as Aretha Franklin not an immediate success?

In part, Franklin's career was limited by the imaginations of music executives at the time. Many followed a formula with certain artists. There was a perception of what kind of songs African-American female vocalists would sing, and they were packaging Franklin in that same style. The industry was, by and large, still segregated, as were its audiences. R&B music was most often recorded by African-American artists and packaged for black audiences. Almost exclusively, black listeners tuned into radio stations that specialized in R&B. White musicians were beginning to listen to R&B and borrow from that sound, but they would make their own versions of the songs to release to white audiences.

Due to the success of Motown and artists such as the Supremes and Dionne Warwick, however, performers were beginning to test those boundaries. Columbia decided to attempt to move Franklin in that direction by having her record contemporary music, instead of the standards that had formed the basis of her repertoire up until then. The new album, *Runnin' Out of Fools*, released in 1964, proved that Aretha's voice was effective in other genres—including rock, pop, and R&B—but because Columbia lacked experience in marketing that style of music, sales of the album were disappointing.

Franklin was also frustrated with some of the songs the label selected for her to record. Ballads were frustrating because the lush backup sound often required her to hold back the sheer power of her voice. And while she had written several songs in her six years of recording for Columbia, only four of her original numbers were ever included in her albums.

Family friend Louise Bishop, a Philadelphia disc jockey, recalled in the book *I Never Loved a Man the Way I Love You* that she was disappointed at the Aretha Franklin she heard in the Columbia recordings. Having heard the teenaged Aretha pouring out her heart in gospel music at New Bethel, and having loved the sound in her first gospel album, Bishop said, "She was obviously with people who didn't really know gospel and didn't hear the gospel that was in 'Retha or the soul that was in 'Retha. She was to some degree *contained*. Knowing her as a gospel singer, I just felt that something was missing."

Franklin's career was at a crossroads. She was in her early twenties and the mother of three young boys. She was working hard, touring and recording. But success still seemed far away.

A FRESH APPROACH

Louise Bishop would help Franklin move her career in a new direction. In early 1966, Franklin was booked for a series of performances at the Cadillac Club in Philadelphia, Pennsylvania, where Bishop was then working as a disc jockey. It was a small venue, with a maximum seating capacity of about 250 people. She sang there for nearly a week, and Bishop attended every performance.

Franklin had added some contemporary numbers to her song list. One of these was a song recorded by singer Otis Redding: "Respect." Redding's version of the song was more soulful, but Franklin, in her version of the song, infused it with a hint of the power she had demonstrated as a gospel singer. When she would later record it, the song would become one of her signature numbers, but at the time it was simply a song she had added to give a more contemporary flavor to her act.

On the last night of the performances, Bishop approached Franklin to offer her a suggestion. "You're an artist!" Bishop recalled saying in *I Never Loved a Man the Way I Love You.* "I know somebody. Why don't you let me introduce you?"

The "somebody" Bishop knew was Jerry Wexler, a writer, promoter, and producer who, with Ahmet Ertegun, served as co-head of Atlantic Records, an independent label that was popularizing the sound of rhythm and blues. (Wexler, in fact, has been described by *Rolling Stone* as "the man who invented rhythm and blues.") Wexler had worked with Ray Charles, Otis Redding, and the Drifters. Later, he would work with Led Zeppelin, Bob Dylan, Dire Straits, and Willie Nelson.

Aretha Franklin and her producer Jerry Wexler receive their gold records for their hit single "I Never Loved A Man (The Way I Love You)" in New York City, in 1967. Theirs would prove to be a very fruitful collaboration.

Wexler was very familiar with Aretha Franklin. He had been impressed by the power and emotion of her early gospel recording "Precious Lord," but was confused by Columbia's decision to package her as a performer of standards. "I knew all her records, and I knew all about her. I was just waiting for her contract to run out," Wexler recalled in *I Never Loved a Man the Way I Love You.* When Bishop contacted him to let him know that Franklin's contract with Columbia was about to expire and she was interested in talking to him, he quickly phoned her.

Meeting Franklin in person, Wexler was struck by her beauty and intelligence. She in turn loved the type of music Atlantic Records was producing. "I wanted a hit," she recalled in her autobiography, "and I wanted to be with a company that understood the current market. Right from the start, I felt good about the arrangement." Franklin, her husband/ manager Ted White, and Wexler quickly came to an agreement. Aretha would get a contract with Atlantic and a $30,000 signing bonus.

From the beginning, Wexler wanted to build the music around Franklin's unique and powerful sound, rather than trying to plug her into a particular existing style or format. She recalled visiting his home, meeting his children and wife, and spending hours listening to different songs and searching for the right material. Perhaps more importantly, Wexler involved her in each decision, seeking her input and approval. "[Jerry] wanted to base the music around me," she remembered in *Aretha: From These Roots,* "not only my feeling for the song but my piano playing and basic rhythm arrangement, my overall concept."

Wexler's plan was for Franklin to record her music at the Muscle Shoals Studio in northwest Alabama. Wexler had enjoyed success recording there with Otis Redding and felt that the Southern flavor from the Alabama musicians he had recruited to help with the recording would enable Franklin to return to the passion and power of the gospel sound that had initially brought her to his attention.

Ted White, however, was reluctant to record in Alabama. In the 1960s, Alabama had become identified with some of the worst cases of racial conflicts and violence. Only three years earlier, in 1963, segregation protests had led to a church bombing that killed four African-American girls in Birmingham. In Selma, white segregationists had beaten and killed a black minister in 1965, triggering widespread protests.

But Wexler felt strongly that Franklin needed to move away from the polished sound Columbia had produced using New York studio musicians. He believed the Alabama musicians could provide a background sound that was slightly rawer, more relaxed and funky, but still professional. Franklin was ready for a change. She had quietly been working on several songs herself, including a song by one of her husband's clients, "I Never Loved a Man (The Way I Love You)."

More than anything, she wanted a hit and trusted Wexler to help her make one. She would record in Alabama.

5

Respect

In order to prepare for Aretha Franklin's debut on Atlantic Records, Wexler had hired a group of Southern studio musicians to work with her—those who he thought would be able to bring out a new sound. Young and ambitious, they included keyboardist Spooner Oldham, rhythm guitarist Jimmy Johnson, bassist David Hood, and drummer Roger Hawkins. In many of the sessions, Franklin herself played the piano.

Franklin had never met the musicians before her arrival at Muscle Shoals; a few of them knew her from her recordings, but most had never even heard of her. Some were not sure how to pronounce her name. At their first meeting in January 1967, she was a bit shy but professional and prepared. The idea was to make music; no one wanted to waste time.

Several of the arrangements were done on the spot in a kind of creative and free-flowing way, with the musicians testing out sounds and adding them in that moment. Songs were recorded on tape; then the musicians, Franklin, and Wexler would listen to what had been recorded on big speakers in the studio. The sound was not a true projection of what the music would sound like on the radio, so next they would all crowd into the control booth to listen to the recording on its smaller speakers. Franklin loved what she heard. "This new Aretha music was raw and real and so much more myself," she wrote in her autobiography.

Singer/songwriter Dan Penn was at that first session and has a clear memory of how Franklin quickly got everyone's attention at their first meeting. In *I Never Loved a Man the Way I Love You*, he recalled:

> Suddenly, she walks over to the piano, she sits down at the piano stool, and I'm watchin' her. She kinda looks around, like, Nobody's watchin' me. I thought she thought for just a second, Is this not my session? And with all the talent she had, she just hit this unknown chord. Kind of kawunka-kawunka-kawung! Like a bell ringing. And every musician in the room stopped what they were doing, went to their guitars and started tunin' up. . . . This girl's at the piano—you were aware that no one could hit that chord. She did it in a very shy way. She didn't do it like, Hey I'm here! It was just her magic.

Wexler's philosophy was that, if a singer could play an instrument, he or she should play that instrument as a part of the recording. Whether or not the musician was the best at the instrument did not matter, Wexler believed. The music he or she produced would add to the sound, giving a personal flavor.

Aretha Franklin was good at the piano, and her sound was as unique as her voice, influenced by the gospel songs she had played as a girl. The chord she hit—possibly just as a way of testing the piano—immediately signaled to the studio musicians that she had come to make music, and that her music would have a unique and powerful sound.

The first song the musicians were to record was "I Never Loved a Man (the Way I Loved You)," a song that had been written by Ted White's client, Ronnie Shannon. The plan was for the musicians to listen to a basic demo of the song, and then Franklin would play and sing a version and gradually the musicians would build their parts around her. Listening to the demo, however, the musicians were underwhelmed. It was a slow song; the lyrics—about heartbreak and a cheating man—were depressing.

But Franklin had been working on the song at home, before traveling to Alabama. She had a rough idea of what she wanted to do, and after the demo had been shut off and she sat down at the piano and began to play, the musicians began to feel more encouraged. Franklin's voice was powerful, and the vocals had been polished from plenty of practice. The musicians, listening to her play, had a sense of the tempo (speed) of the music and the key in which it was going to be played.

Wexler later noted how challenging this type of recording could be for musicians. "[Aretha] has her own harmonic concept, where she can go from blues to gospel," he said in *I Never Loved a Man the Way I Love You*. "She has a very interesting way of melding, mixing up blues chords and gospel chords, which throws the musicians off, until they get to learn the progression. . . . She's got her own time."

After listening to Franklin breathe life into what seemed to be a fairly standard blues song, the musicians gradually began to add their own unique contributions. It began with the Wurlitzer electric piano, which echoed the opening keyboard pattern played by Aretha. Then the drummer gradually sensed the rhythm. Slowly, a bluesy bass sound was added. The result was a sound almost like a waltz in rhythm. Gradually, she made the decision that the song would work better if she held off playing the piano until the second verse. Parts were quickly written for a horn section, and those musicians began to play. The musical arrangement was created and the song recorded

The LP album cover for Aretha Franklin's *I Never Loved A Man The Way I Loved You*, released in 1967. Her Atlantic Records label debut is considered by fans and critics to be an indisputable masterpiece, due in large part to producer Jerry Wexler, who allowed the singer's soulful voice to flourish.

in the same day. In fact, the song took only a few hours to record in roughly three or four final takes.

CONFLICT IN THE STUDIO

The experience of working on that first song was extraordinary for the musicians present. Unfortunately, after that first recording a conflict erupted between a trumpet player and Ted White. Franklin, in her autobiography, states that the details of this dispute are no longer clear in her memory. Matt Dobkin, in *I Never Loved a Man the Way I Loved You*, quotes Ted White as saying that the dispute happened because the trumpet player was behaving in a way he felt was disrespectful to Franklin.

While tensions were high between some of the players, Franklin and a few others were already working on a second song. Dan Penn had brought with him a rough demo of a song he and a partner had written—a song called "Do Right Woman"—but it was still unfinished and he was roughing out the lyrics in the background. He played the demo for Jerry Wexler, who loved it but asked him to polish the song and add a new section. This new section was missing lyrics, so Penn supplied the first line ("They say it's a man's world") and Wexler added the second ("But you can't prove that by me"). Franklin, checking on their progress to see if they were ready to start work on the new song, added the next line when they were stuck: "As long as we're together baby, show some respect for me."

The plan was to record an album's worth of songs in a week. But Franklin needed a bit more time on that first day to get a feel for "Do Right Woman." Because she had only heard it a few hours earlier, she needed to practice it before recording began. The plan was to continue work on the song and record it the next day. But when tomorrow came, Franklin and White had left Alabama and the session was canceled. White was furious at the dispute with the horn player; Franklin was upset that the fight between her husband and a musician had disrupted the earlier positive atmosphere in the studio.

It took Wexler two weeks to track Franklin down and persuade her to resume work on the album. This time the recording was moved from Alabama to Atlantic Records' New York studio. The musicians from Muscle Shoals were brought north for the sessions. Aretha's sisters, Erma and Carolyn, were hired as backup singers, as was Cissy Houston, the mother of future pop singer Whitney Houston.

In the meantime, Wexler leaked some early recordings of "I Never Loved a Man" to a few of his DJ friends, including Louise Bishop. The response was overwhelming, and the pressure increased for an album to be completed so that the single—and others—could be released.

Dan Penn was astonished when he first heard what Franklin had done with his song "Do Right Woman," on which she plays piano and her sisters sing backup. "It was just amazing," he recalled in *I Never Loved a Man the Way I Love You.* "I really thought, on that day, that that was the best record I ever heard. Not just cause it was my song—I just liked the record. It was beautiful. I still wonder what kind of talent it takes to pull that together. It took *some*, and she's got it." "Do Right Woman" and "Save Me," a more upbeat number, were the first to be recorded in New York.

"RESPECT"

Franklin suggested adding "Respect" to the list of songs for the new album. On February 14, 1967, Valentine's Day, the group recorded the song that would become one of her signature numbers. The song would become not only an anthem for the singer herself, but also for many women and for all those demanding to be taken seriously. It spoke to the emotions of the civil rights movement. In many ways, it was the perfect song for its era.

Franklin had performed it earlier, while on tour, and had a clear sense of the rhythm and piano arrangements, which gave it a feel that was quite different from the version Otis Redding had initially recorded. The studio musicians added their contributions after first listening to her play it on the piano. The guitar player studied her right hand to determine the key and the melody; the bass player watched her left hand to come up with a bass line. Franklin helped oversee the background singers, instructing them in how best to blend with her.

The recording process for "Respect" set a pattern that was followed for the remainder of the numbers on the album. She and the band first performed all of the instrumental music, with Franklin singing a rough version of the vocals simply for the musicians to follow. This would then be replaced with a more polished vocal she recorded separately. Once the musicians had created a final track, she would get up from the piano and go over to a separate microphone set up to record vocals. The musicians would leave the studio and go into the control room and sit down—they were the audience for each take as she worked to perfect the sound. Most often, she insisted on multiple attempts at the vocals until she had a sound that completely satisfied her.

When Franklin finally had a vocal on "Respect" that satisfied her, all involved knew that they had a hit song. Soon after, Wexler called Otis Redding, who had first recorded "Respect," and played Franklin's version for him. "Looks like that little gal done took my song," Redding declared, according to Matt Dobkin.

In a single day of recording, Franklin produced "Respect" as well as covers of Ray Charles's "Drown in My Own Tears" and her friend Sam Cooke's "A Change Is Gonna Come." "Drown in My Own Tears" showcases the mix of blues and gospel that had been Wexler's inspiration when he first conceived of highlighting Franklin's voice in a new way. The day also included two songs she herself had cowritten: "Don't Let Me Lose This Dream" (with her husband) and "Baby, Baby, Baby" (with her sister Carolyn).

On the third and final day of recording, "Dr. Feelgood," "Soul Serenade," and "Good Times" by Sam Cooke were recorded, and the album—to be titled *I Never Loved a Man the Way I Love You*—was completed. In her autobiography, Aretha states that soul was the key to each of the numbers in her debut album for

Atlantic Records. "There was no compromising," she said, "no deliberate decision to go pop. As it turned out, these records crossed over and sold on the charts. But we weren't trying to manipulate or execute any marketing plan. We were simply trying to compose real music from my heart."

THE SOUND OF AN ERA

The first singles from the album, "I Never Loved a Man" and "Do Right Woman," were released on February 10, 1967,

Otis Redding

Otis Redding was born in 1941 in Macon, Georgia. He was discovered while singing in Macon with the Pinetoppers, and in 1960 he first recorded as a member of that group. Two years later, when the lead guitarist of the group was booked to record some songs in Memphis for Stax Records, Redding went with him and, at the end of the session, had a chance to record a solo number. He picked a ballad he had written, "These Arms of Mine." Redding's talent was quickly recognized, and he was signed to Stax Records, whose music was being distributed by Atlantic under the supervision of Jerry Wexler.

Redding became a key contributor to the development of soul music at Stax Records in the 1960s, although his only number-one hit—"(Sittin' on) the Dock of the Bay"—came after his death. His voice was rich and gravelly. Many of the songs he recorded were numbers he had written. A talented guitarist, he also assisted in the arrangements for his music, whistling parts to show the other musicians what they were supposed to play. He recorded one album—*Otis Blue/Otis Redding Sings Soul*—in a single, 24-hour period in 1965. Such songs as "Respect," "I've Been Loving You Too Long," and "Try a Little Tenderness" became iconic examples of soul music.

Redding's career was tragically cut short when he died in a plane crash in 1967 at the age of 26. In 1989, he was inducted into the Rock and Roll Hall of Fame, where he is described as "a singer of such commanding stature that to this day he embodies the essence of soul music in its purist form."

before the entire album had been recorded. The album *I Never Loved a Man the Way I Loved You* was released in March. On March 25 (Aretha's twenty-fifth birthday), the single "I Never Loved a Man (The Way I Love You)" reached number one on the R&B charts. It would go as high as number nine on the pop charts.

Two months later, "Respect" was played on the airwaves and quickly soared to the top of both the R&B and pop charts, signaling that Aretha Franklin's music was speaking to both

Soul singer Otis Redding performs on a British television show in London, England, in 1966. Aretha Franklin's version of Redding's "Respect" would later be not only a huge hit for her, but is considered one of the great pop singles of all time.

white and black audiences. In just a few weeks, it sold a million copies. Her dream of becoming a successful recording artist finally was coming true.

There was, however, little time to relish her success. While today musicians often wait two or three years between albums, in the 1960s musicians were expected to release a new album every five or six months. In August 1967, a new album, *Aretha Arrives*, was in stores, and the single "Baby, I Love You" was on its way to being another million-seller. With Franklin's songs tearing up the charts, all of the top clubs wanted to book her. Even the prestigious Apollo Theater was interested.

Franklin focused carefully on her appearances and determined to agree only to certain select concerts, eager to protect her voice and also her image from overexposure. She paid more attention to fashion, wanting to ensure that her costumes and outfits for her concerts were special. Her attention to detail worked. She soon appeared on *The Tonight Show*, and *Billboard* selected her as the top female singer of 1967.

MARTIN LUTHER KING JR.

In February 1968, Mayor James Cavanaugh of Detroit declared February 16 to be Aretha Franklin Day. As part of the celebration, Franklin performed in Cobo Hall to a crowd of some 12,000 screaming and cheering fans. As a surprise, Dr. Martin Luther King Jr., who as previously mentioned was her father's friend, attended the performance. Although King was heavily involved in the civil rights movement, he took the time to attend the concert and present her with a special honor, the Drum Beat Award, from the organization he headed, the Southern Christian Leadership Conference (SCLC). The award was a thank you for the many performances she had given in the past on behalf of the organization. He asked her to sing one of his favorite songs, the gospel tune "Precious Lord," which she had first recorded at the age of 14.

Less than two months later, King was assassinated in Memphis. Franklin flew to his funeral. She visited briefly with his widow, Coretta Scott King, and then returned home. A few weeks later, at a televised SCLC conference in Memphis, Franklin sang a musical tribute to King, performing the song that was his favorite gospel tune, the song he had asked her to sing on Aretha Franklin Day. The words of "Precious Lord" rang out over those gathered, full of new meaning and emotion in the wake of King's death.

6

Queen of Soul

By 1968, Aretha Franklin's career was skyrocketing. Chicago disc jockey Pervis Spann hosted a special ceremony for her at the Regal Theater. During the ceremony, Spann placed a crown on her head and dubbed her the "Queen of Soul." It is a name that she had earned.

In addition to her successful singles, albums, and performances, Franklin appeared on the cover of *Time* in June 1968. In an article titled "Lady Soul Singing It Like It Is," the magazine praised the "fierce, gritty conviction" audible in her music. "She does not seem to be performing," the author of the article wrote, "so much as bearing witness to a reality so simple and compelling that she could not possibly fake it."

The magazine article described a young woman whose life was professionally successful but personally unhappy and hinted at possible domestic violence in her relationship with Ted White. While she had bought a comfortable home in

Aretha Franklin performs at the 1968 Democratic National Convention in Chicago, Illinois. In the late 1960s and early 1970s, Franklin enjoyed extraordinary commercial success.

Detroit, where she was living with her three sons, her circle of friends was small and she had little time for expanding it, since much of her time was spent recording, rehearsing, or preparing for appearances.

Today, Franklin contends that many of the points printed in the article were untrue and that her comments on her personal life were taken out of context. The article, however, was accurate in its reporting that her relationship with White was damaged. Soon after its publication, the couple decided to divorce.

Franklin's third album for Atlantic, *Lady Soul*, was released in January 1968. Two of its songs would become closely identified with Franklin: "Chain of Fools" and "(You Make Me Feel Like) A Natural Woman." The album contains songs written by Carolyn Franklin ("Ain't No Way") and by Franklin herself ("Since You've Been Gone"). And it includes her covers of songs recorded by other artists, including "Come Back Baby" by Ray Charles, "Groovin'" by the Young Rascals, "People Get Ready" by Curtis Mayfield, and "Money Won't Change You" by James Brown.

By June 1968, a fourth album, *Aretha Now*, was in the stores. It contains more explosive numbers, including "Think" and "I Can't See Myself Leaving You." After having recorded four albums in less than two years, Franklin felt she had enough material to begin preparing for a tour of Europe, where she would travel to France, Germany, Holland, Switzerland, and the United Kingdom. Her next album, *Aretha in Paris* (1968), recorded at the Olympia Theatre, contains 13 live versions of music that she performed in the French capital.

Two months later, in August, Franklin was back in the United States to perform at the 1968 Democratic National Convention, held in Chicago. The convention would be marked by violence and protests against the Vietnam War, but her performance of "The Star-Spangled Banner" was a high point of the otherwise marred political gathering.

KEN CUNNINGHAM

In 1969, Franklin met Ken Cunningham, a businessman, in Miami. He had arranged the meeting to see if the singer might be interested in investing in a business venture featuring black clothing designers. The couple fell in love; a year later they had a son together, who they named Kecalf (a combination of the couple's initials—Ken E. Cunningham and Aretha Louise Franklin), pronounced "Kelf."

The relationship inspired Franklin to relocate to New York City since the clothing manufacturing operation Cunningham was overseeing was based nearby. Soon, she and Cunningham were living in a luxurious penthouse apartment on the thirtieth floor of a high-rise building. The two-level apartment had three bedrooms and Franklin had a piano near a window overlooking Manhattan. When Kecalf was born, he lived with his parents, but Franklin's other sons alternated time with her, living in both New York and Detroit. While Franklin's grandmother raised her two eldest sons, Clarence and Eddie, Teddy lived with his father, Ted White, and White's mother.

Now comfortably settled in New York, Franklin began to experiment with people's expectations of her. In 1969, Aretha returned to a jazz big band sound on her album *Soul '69*, which features covers of several American standards and also songs made famous by Smokey Robinson and country singer Glen Campbell. Franklin's look was also changing. Inspired by Cunningham, she began to wear more natural makeup and style her hair in an Afro. "I began to appreciate myself as a beautiful black woman," she wrote in her autobiography. Cunningham introduced her to African art, poetry, and sculpture. A second album released in 1969, *Aretha's Gold*, was primarily a collection of her hits from 1967 and 1968, but there was also one new song, "The House That Jack Built."

In late 1969, Aretha returned to the studio to record the songs that would form the basis of *This Girl's in Love with You*, released in 1970. The album featured two songs written by The Beatles,

Aretha Franklin poses with her son Kecalf in Los Angeles, California, on January 17, 1981. Ken Cunningham, Kecalf's father, inspired Franklin to experiment musically and stylistically.

"Let It Be" and "Eleanor Rigby." Another song on the album, "Share Your Love with Me," earned her a fourth Grammy. The record also featured one of her own compositions, "Call Me," a song based on her relationship with Cunningham.

Later in 1970, Franklin released *Spirit in the Dark*. Four singles from that album—"Call Me," "Spirit in the Dark," "Don't Play That Song for Me," and "Border Song"—became top-10 hits on the R&B charts, and "Don't Play That Song for Me" brought her another Grammy. The album includes a song written by Franklin, "Try Matty's," which was a tribute to a soul-food restaurant in northwest Detroit that featured ribs she loved.

LIVE AT THE FILLMORE WEST

For part of each year, Franklin traveled to Florida. Jerry Wexler had set up a studio in Miami where, during the winter, she could record songs. She was happy, enjoying a successful run of hit singles, but eager to have a number-one album.

In 1971, Wexler arranged an unusual appearance for Franklin, a concert at the Fillmore West in San Francisco, California. At the time, San Francisco was home to a large number of hippies—young Americans who were part of the counterculture protest movement and were identified by their long hair and nontraditional clothing (such as jeans and tie-dyed shirts). Hippies tended to prefer psychedelic rock music and such bands as The Grateful Dead over Franklin's trademark sound, and the Fillmore West was a premiere venue for such acts.

Franklin was 28 years old when she performed at Fillmore West. To appeal to the expected audience, she chose a series of rock and roll numbers, as well as more rock-influenced versions of some of her hits. Because of the unique nature of the concert, Atlantic Records decided to record the concert live for an album.

Before the performance, Franklin was concerned that the concert might be a flop, but when she arrived the hall was packed with three times its normal capacity and the crowd responded enthusiastically to her music. She performed "Love the One You're With," "Bridge Over Troubled Water," and "Eleanor Rigby" for this particular audience, but their warmest response came when she was joined onstage by legendary performer Ray Charles, with whom she sang her recent single "Spirit in the Dark." Charles did not know all of the lyrics, but he added his own ad-libs, which brought a special emotion to the performance. "All the planets were aligned right that night," she recalled in her autobiography, "because when the music came down, it was as real and righteous as any recording I'd ever made." Wexler, in the audience that night, was overwhelmed by the audience's response to his star. In his memoir *Rhythm and the Blues*, he said, "All I could do was sit there and weep."

After *Aretha Live at Fillmore West* was released in 1971, it became a top-10 album. As Franklin noted in *Aretha: From These Roots*, "It was a night to remember."

RETURN TO GOSPEL

The early 1970s represented a time of growing independence for Aretha Franklin. She and Ken Cunningham roamed throughout the world. They spent time exploring the Caribbean and the Bahamas. They vacationed in Barbados and Bermuda. They traveled to Venezuela, to England and Italy, to the French Riviera and Spain.

The couple moved from their penthouse apartment to an elegant four-story brownstone townhouse on Manhattan's exclusive Upper East Side, which Franklin furnished with artifacts from France and Egypt and other souvenirs from their global travels. Cunningham introduced Franklin to many different cuisines, and they ate in Cuban, Greek, and Italian restaurants throughout New York. She also briefly studied dance at the Academy of Ballet, in an effort to incorporate more elaborate dance routines into her performances.

Though Franklin had experimented with many different styles of music throughout her career, in 1972 she decided to return to the music that she had sung at the beginning: gospel. Jerry Wexler supported the plan. After the success of *Aretha Live at Fillmore West,* he had wanted to do another live album with her. Together, they decided that the album would be recorded in a church.

It was an opportunity for Franklin to reconnect not only with the style of music that had shaped her sound, but also with old friends. She chose to make the recording at New Temple Missionary Baptist Church in Los Angeles, where her old choir director, James Cleveland, was leading the Southern California Community Choir. Several of the musicians she had used on previous recordings for Atlantic traveled with her for the recording, but Franklin was clear that there needed to be a real congregation present. "Gospel is a living music," she wrote in *Aretha: From These Roots,* "and it comes most alive during an actual service."

Franklin also invited her father and her old mentor, Clara Ward, as honored guests. For two separate nights they recorded, and the audience responded with cheers and cries of "Amen!" She performed many of the songs she had sung as a girl, including "How I Got Over," an extended 10-minute version of "Amazing Grace," and "Never Grow Old." James Cleveland joined her for a duet on "Precious Memories." She also included some contemporary songs, such as Marvin Gaye's "Wholy Holy" and Carole King's "You've Got a Friend."

At the end of the service, her father stood up and addressed the congregation. She recalled his words in her autobiography:

> Aretha and James took me all the way back to the living room at home when she was six and seven years of age. I saw you crying . . . and I saw you respond . . . but I was just about to bust wide open . . . you talk about being moved. Not only because Aretha is my daughter, Aretha is just a

stone singer . . . if you want to know the truth, she has never left the church.

C.L. Franklin's comment about his daughter never having "left the church" was an important one to her. Many gospel singers had experienced resentment from their former admirers when they attempted to cross over and begin recording popular music, and few returned to gospel songs after they had experienced success with other forms of music. Aretha Franklin's decision to record a gospel album was a courageous one. It was a way of demonstrating her continued love for the songs she had sung as a girl, and the style of music she had first recorded. But the experience was as much a commercial success as it was a personal one. The resulting live album, *Amazing Grace* (1972), which was the first to list her as co-producer, earned Franklin her eighth Grammy Award (in the category of Best Soul Gospel) and went gold (meaning it had sold a half-million copies).

CHANGES

At this time, Ken Cunningham was becoming increasingly involved with Franklin's career. He shot the photo that appeared on the cover of *Amazing Grace*, in which she wore a sample of the African-style clothing his designers were creating. He also helped design the artwork for the cover of her next album, *Hey Now Hey*, released in 1973. That album—Franklin's twelfth for Atlantic Records—featured more of a jazz flavor, the result of her collaboration with legendary producer Quincy Jones. Such songs as "Moody's Mood" and "Just Right Tonight" highlight her experimentation with jazz sounds and styling, while her own compositions include the title song, "Hey Now Hey," as well as "Sister from Texas" and "Master of Eyes." Her sister Carolyn contributed one of the album's more successful singles, the haunting "Angel."

Despite her professional success, conflict was simmering behind the scenes between Ken Cunningham and Franklin's brother, Cecil, who had been serving as her manager. Before agreeing to support his sister as her manager, Cecil had served as a pastor at New Bethel Baptist with his father and had little professional experience in the music business. Cunningham's interference with decisions made by Cecil added tension to his relationship with Franklin.

In those years, Franklin lost two women who had been important mentors for her. In 1973, Clara Ward died at the age of 48. She had been a source of support and encouragement for Aretha in her early years and had helped to popularize gospel music in a new way. At her funeral in Philadelphia, Franklin sang the Clara Ward song, "The Day Is Past and Gone," which she had sung as a 14-year-old on her first gospel album. Just a year earlier, in 1972, gospel singer Mahalia Jackson had died. Franklin was also invited to sing at her funeral service.

Aretha Franklin had proven that she could be successful singing pop or gospel, recording original music or standards made famous by other artists. She had earned numerous industry awards, and the success of her albums and concerts had made her a wealthy woman. For an astonishing eight straight years, she had won a Grammy for Best R&B Performance, Female.

In 1974, Franklin released a new album, the first studio record on which she would receive co-producing credit. Like previous recordings, *Let Me in Your Life* featured a number of standout tracks, including the hit song "Until You Come Back to Me (That's What I'm Gonna Do)," written for her by Stevie Wonder. The single "Ain't Nothing Like the Real Thing" brought her another Grammy, her tenth.

But popular musical tastes were changing in the mid-1970s. Disco was increasingly replacing R&B on many radio stations. The next two albums Franklin released, *With Everything I Feel in Me* (1974) and *You* (1975), met with disappointing results. And her relationship with Ken Cunningham was also struggling. She decided that a move might help her career and her relationship. Because she had loved the weather and the atmosphere in California since the days of her road trips with her father to the Golden State, she decided to move to Los Angeles.

Franklin settled into a home in the San Fernando Valley near the Walt Disney estate, a short drive from Hollywood and Beverly Hills. It had a pool, and a brook ran through the center of the property. In her autobiography, she mentions that she became a little too comfortable settling into domestic life in California and enjoying some of the area's best restaurants. She was also smoking too much and not spending enough time exercising or caring for her health.

A concert in Pittsburgh provided a wake-up call. Halfway into the concert, Franklin discovered that she was out of breath and unable to sustain the long, powerful notes that were her trademark. Alarmed, she enrolled in dance classes in

IN HER OWN WORDS...

In the mid-1970s, as disco music was increasing in popularity, many artists who were identified with rhythm and blues or soul saw their careers falter. Aretha addressed this period in her career in her autobiography, *Aretha: From These Roots*:

> I take this business of soul music seriously; a song, like a person, must have a soul. I realized that my voice would have worked with disco tracks. But I was determined not to be labeled a disco artist. I'm in the music industry for the long run. No matter how much the radio stations were shoving rhythm and blues back in the corner, I still believed and I believe today in the permanent value and staying power of soul music. Soul music is cultural, and it should forever be enshrined as one of the world's greatest forms of music. It is a people, a nation, and it is the rhythm of our lives and loves and losses and wins, our hopes and dreams and passions on parade. Like jazz and gospel, it is a musical strain that will live forever because it is born out of real emotions and people's experiences. R&B isn't a fad; it's the truth.

Los Angeles and began exercising regularly, slowly rebuilding her strength and stamina.

While Franklin was happy in California, Cunningham was not. After he returned to New York, the two gradually drifted apart. At the same time, Aretha enjoyed some brief success with the 1976 album *Sparkle*, a soundtrack to a film of the same name that told the story of a girl group from the ghetto rising to fame. With songs written by Curtis Mayfield, the soundtrack brought Franklin back to a bluesy R&B sound. *Sparkle* also contained another hit single for Franklin, "Something He Can Feel."

But the popularity of the disco sound continued to challenge Franklin's career. She attempted to launch a line of clothing, meeting with different designers to explore her ideas about fashion, but the project never got off the ground. She performed at the Oscars and at the pre-inaugural gala for President Jimmy Carter in 1977. She also lent her distinctive voice to commercials for Yellow Pages and Armour hot dogs.

Aretha Franklin was searching for her next step. But that next step would come not in her professional life, but in her personal one.

7

Jump to It

While performing at a benefit in 1977, Aretha Franklin was introduced to Glynn Turman, a stage actor who had recently starred in such movies as *Cooley High* and *Five on the Black Hand Side.* Glynn was 12 years younger than Franklin and the father of three children; she had her four sons. At first, the couple initially decided to simply be friends, but by the end of the year Turman proposed and she accepted.

After several unsuccessful relationships, Franklin was determined to have the wedding of her dreams. Her father would marry her at his church, New Bethel Baptist. She began planning the Detroit ceremony, with a reception to be held the next day in Beverly Hills for friends there. The ceremony, held on April 11, 1978, was a glittering affair. Crowds lined the streets outside the church, chanting "Aretha, Aretha" as she went by. Photographers snapped pictures. Franklin wore a silk gown (with an eight-foot train) trimmed in fur and decorated with thousands of hand-sewn pearls. The Four Tops sang Stevie Wonder's "Isn't She Lovely," and her sister Carolyn sang a song she had written especially for the wedding, "I Take This Walk with Thee." A full choir sang the gospel hymns she had loved as a child, and there was an eight-foot, four-tier wedding cake. In Los Angeles, 500 guests attended the reception. Yet not all went perfectly that day. Years later, she fumed in her autobiography that one of the bridesmaids tried to upstage her by wearing a see-through dress.

After the wedding, the couple moved into a new, larger home in Los Angeles. Her personal life was full and happy. But her professional life was unsatisfying. She had released several albums that had failed to become gold. She felt that Atlantic Records was no longer doing a satisfactory job promoting and marketing her music. Jerry Wexler had already left the company, depriving her of a fruitful collaboration. After 12 years and 19 albums, she felt that she, too, was ready for a change.

The team at Arista Records, under the direction of Clive Davis, had impressed Franklin with the way they were managing careers of successful pop music artists such as Barry Manilow, Dionne Warwick, and Melissa Manchester. Although Davis had once worked at Franklin's old label Columbia, he and Franklin had not worked together during that period. Arista was a label Davis had started on his own and built on his own. After a meeting with Davis, she was impressed by his intelligence and appreciation of music. Franklin decided that the time had come to sign with a new label.

In addition to signing with Arista, Franklin had an opportunity to take her career in a direction she had always wanted to try: acting. She had become especially interested in acting after attending several of the acting workshops her new husband led in Los Angeles, although she, admittedly, had not really enjoyed his uninhibited style of inspiring his students.

Ahmet Ertegun

While Aretha Franklin was at Atlantic Records, she initially worked with Jerry Wexler. Later, after Wexler left the label, she worked with the chairman of Atlantic Records, Ahmet Ertegun, who had co-founded the label in 1947 with a $10,000 loan from a dentist. In the early postwar period, there were many small independent labels. Typically, each of them churned out a few hits, maybe produced a star or two, and then disappeared. But by the 1960s, Atlantic Records had defied the independent label curse. With Ertegun as its chairman, the label was a huge success. Boasting such stars as Aretha Franklin, Ray Charles, Led Zeppelin, and The Rolling Stones, Atlantic Records was producing many of the artists who were defining music in the 1960s and 1970s.

Ertegun was the son of a Turkish diplomat. Educated in European schools, he eventually moved to Washington, D.C. In that city, which was segregated when he first moved there, he discovered jazz and began searching for obscure clubs in which he could listen to jazz and, later, R&B. Many labels, especially in the 1950s, were producing music specifically for teenagers. Ertegun ensured that Atlantic Records would produce music for adults, music with a particular clarity and quality that made its recordings stand out from those of its competitors.

The Muslim-raised Ertegun brought a gospel sound to the label; in fact, many of the artists signed to Atlantic, including Franklin, had performed gospel music early in their careers. After the 1950s, he focused more on the business end than the hands-on work as a producer. But he relished the artists he hired, socialized with them, and attended their concerts. These friendships, however, did not interfere with his ability to keep his eye on the bottom line. When both Franklin and, later, The Rolling Stones received higher offers from competing labels, he was willing to let them leave rather than pay them more than he thought he should.

Later in life, Ertegun was deeply involved in the effort to start the Rock and Roll Hall of Fame and Museum. The *New York Times* quoted him as saying that he hoped that his legacy would be that "I did a little bit to raise the dignity and recognition of the greatness of African-American music."

Ertegun died on December 14, 2006 at the age of 83 from injuries sustained from a fall backstage shortly before a Rolling Stones concert. At the time of his death, he was still serving as chairman of Atlantic Records.

Ahmet Ertegun sits behind his desk in his office at Atlantic Records in New York City, on February 2, 2005. Ertegun helped define American music as the founder of Atlantic Records, a label that popularized the gritty R&B of Ray Charles, the classic soul of Aretha Franklin, and the British rock of The Rolling Stones.

In 1979, Franklin was offered a part in *The Blues Brothers,* a comedy starring John Belushi and Dan Ackroyd. Her scene would prove one of the most memorable in the movie. Playing a restaurant owner whose husband is about to leave her to join the Blues Brothers band, she delivered her lines with relish. Her appearance in the film concluded with a full version of

Aretha Franklin in her scene-stealing performance in *The Blues Brothers* (1980), starring, from left, Dan Ackroyd and Jim Belushi.

"Think," her 1968 hit song. The movie was an enormous success, and she received positive reviews for her performance.

PERSONAL TRAGEDY

It was June 1979. Franklin was booked at the Aladdin Hotel in Las Vegas. She had just completed the first performance of the evening when she noticed her brother and husband waiting in the wings. After her final number, she walked over to them. Her brother then delivered the devastating news that their father had been shot.

Franklin later learned that burglars had broken into her father's home looking for money. During the course of the robbery, C.L. Franklin had encountered the burglars and been shot twice. Neighbors who heard the gunfire and saw people running from the house had discovered him and called an ambulance. He had survived the shooting but fallen into a coma.

Franklin hurried back to Detroit. Her father would never communicate with her or anyone again. He would remain in a coma for five years before passing away on July 27, 1984. For those next few years, Franklin shuttled back and forth between Detroit and Los Angeles. Her sister Carolyn, who had been living with her in California, moved back to Detroit to help their siblings Erma and Cecil care for their father. Because his care, which required round-the-clock nurses, was expensive, Franklin focused her attention on her career in order to earn enough money for his medical needs. In her autobiography, she refers to this time as "perhaps the most difficult in my life." She smoked too much and gained weight.

Franklin's first two albums for Arista—*Aretha* (1980) and *Love All the Hurt Away* (1981)—gave her not only the opportunity to pay for her father's care, but also to reunite with some of her favorite backup musicians and singers. *Aretha* spawned the hit "Can't Turn You Loose," an Otis Redding song from the 1960s, which earned Franklin a Grammy nomination in the category of R&B Vocal Performance, Female. *Love All the Hurt Away* was her first album to score in the Top 40 on *Billboard*'s album charts in six years and brought her an eleventh Grammy.

Arista arranged a concert tour in England, where Franklin sang at a gala command performance in London attended by Prince Charles and Elizabeth, the Queen Mother. During her visit, she met the prince and several other members of the royal family. At home, she was honored for her contributions to music. She was given a star on the Hollywood Walk of Fame, and the world-renowned Joffrey Ballet put together a program featuring Franklin's music, a source of great pride to her.

Then, in 1982, 40-year-old Franklin released *Jump to It*. The lively title track, featuring an ad-libbed conversation between the singer and a friend, became a huge hit and took her back to the top of the charts. R&B singer Luther Vandross produced the title song and would go on to produce the title track on her successful follow-up, *Get It Right* (1983). That album also features "Giving In," a song written by her son Clarence and featuring her son Teddy on guitar. She was back on top.

CHANGES

The stress of commuting between California and Detroit, and concern over her father, wore heavily on Franklin, despite her success. "My family obligation centered on being there for Daddy," she wrote in *Aretha: From These Roots.* "Being there was not easy for any of us. You sat with him and you hoped he was comforted by your presence and knew you were there, but you didn't know."

The stress also took a toll on her marriage. Soon, Franklin and Turman decided to divorce. In 1982, she moved back to her father's home in Detroit, where she shared a room with her sister Carolyn and focused on spending time with her father.

It was in 1983, after a stressful series of appearances and meetings in Atlanta, that Franklin began to experience the fear of flying that has plagued her ever since. She missed her flight and decided to take a smaller two-engine prop plane back to Detroit. She experienced an anxiety attack during the turbulent flight. "I now realize I should have gotten right back into it and taken another flight," she wrote in her autobiography. "I should not have let my fear get the best of me and let so much time go by. But it did." Her fear of flying would impact her tour scheduling, making it impossible for her to appear in concert outside the continental United States. Since that time, she has traveled by custom bus.

Franklin's fear of flying unfortunately cost her a chance to appear on Broadway in a musical based on the life of Mahalia Jackson. She had signed the contracts and had begun learning the music, but when it was time for her to take a plane to New York to begin rehearsals, she experienced another anxiety attack. She decided to drive instead, but the distance between Detroit and New York overwhelmed her. When she decided to back out of the production, she was sued and forced to pay a large sum.

When her father died after spending five years in a coma on July 27, 1984, Franklin grieved, but she was warmed by the outpouring of affection she received. Thousands of people attended his memorial service. More lined the streets outside the church, listening to the service over loudspeakers. Reverend Jesse Jackson, an old family friend, spoke at the funeral. Franklin remembered his words in her autobiography:

> C.L. Franklin was born in 1915, fifty years after slavery, and fifty years before we had the right to vote. He was born in poverty, but poverty could not stop him. He was born in segregation. It was illegal for a black man to get an education. No public accommodations, no right to vote, blacks on chain gangs. No friend in the White House, no black member of Congress, no black mayor. Born in poverty. But when God wants a flower to bloom, no drought can stop it.

WHO'S ZOOMIN' WHO?

After her father's death, Franklin decided to remain in Detroit. She bought a home in the suburbs and an apartment in the city. She also set up a recording studio in the city, so that she could make music close to home.

In 1985, Franklin was impressed with the success of the self-titled debut album by Whitney Houston. Houston was the daughter of Cissy Houston, who had sung backup for Franklin on several of her albums. Narada Michael Walden had produced Houston's album, and when Franklin expressed an interest in working with Walden, Clive Davis at Arista made the arrangements.

Franklin's new album was called *Who's Zoomin' Who?* The phrase was an expression she used to mean "Who's fooling who?" She used it most often when referring to a romantic relationship. Walden liked the expression and decided to set it to music. In addition to the title track, the album also includes a duet with Annie Lennox of the Eurythmics called "Sisters Are Doin' It for Themselves" and an upbeat number called "Freeway of Love" that featured Clarence Clemons of Bruce Springsteen and the E Street Band on the tenor sax.

When *Who's Zoomin' Who?* was released in 1985, it quickly brought Franklin back to the superstar status she had previously enjoyed. In fact, "Sisters Are Doin' It for Themselves" became something of a feminist anthem, celebrating female independence and power. "Freeway of Love" was a pop success, her twentieth single to reach the top of the soul charts. It won a Grammy in 1985 for Best R&B Performance, Female.

"Freeway of Love" also became the first music video Aretha Franklin ever made. Like the album itself, the video was made in Detroit. It was filmed at a Detroit restaurant called Doug's Body Shop, where the décor centered on a car theme (the booths were made from the interiors of classic cars). In the video, she sports a spiky punk hairdo, and in the final scene she drives away in a classic pink Cadillac.

The new success brought Franklin critical praise for her ability, in her forties, to continue to record relevant popular songs. The artist herself was honored in a number of ways. Around this time, a special ceremony was held in Michigan to honor her 25 years in show business. On May 23, 1985, governor James Blanchard of Michigan declared "Aretha Franklin Appreciation Day." "Freeway of Love" became so popular that a section of Detroit's Washington Boulevard was renamed after the song. Moreover, she was hired to endorse several products in television commercials, including Coca-Cola and Dial soap, and she hosted an hour-long television special, *Aretha*, in 1986.

AT HOME IN MICHIGAN

With her return to the top of the charts, Franklin decided to make Detroit her professional base. She bought an expansive, contemporary-style home in a suburb of Detroit, surrounded by trees and fields, where Franklin enjoyed swimming in her pool and puttering in the vegetable garden.

Franklin quickly began work on a new album, which was titled simply *Aretha*. Released in 1986, it included a duet with popular singer George Michael, "I Knew You Were Waiting (for Me)." It also included "Jumpin' Jack Flash," a Rolling Stones' number that featured band members Keith Richards and Ron Wood. In all cases, these musicians traveled to Detroit to record with Franklin.

While Franklin enjoyed the success and opportunities, her father was never far from her thoughts. In 1987, as the third anniversary of his death neared, she decided to honor his memory with a new gospel album. "I wanted to feel the excitement, strength, spirit, and inspiration that comes only in church," she wrote in her autobiography. "I decided that no matter how well my pop records were selling, I owed it to myself and my fans to honor tradition. . . . I felt moved to renew the original musical faith in which I was born."

The experience of recording *Amazing Grace* 15 years earlier had been so powerful that Franklin decided to record this new album as part of a religious service, just as she had done with *Amazing Grace*. She selected New Bethel Baptist, the church once led by her father and now located on C.L. Franklin Boulevard, a street that had been renamed in his honor. Her plan was to enlist the help of family, invite leading gospel artists to perform, select some of her favorite songs, and include some of her favorite ministers. The result was *One Lord, One Faith, One Baptism*, an extraordinary gospel album recorded over three nights in August 1987. The two-record set features both stirring music and impassioned preaching. Gospel artists Mavis and Yvonne Staples appeared on the recording. Franklin

Aretha Franklin performs a gospel number. Throughout her career, Franklin has maintained close ties to her gospel roots, despite her popularity as a soul singer.

sang for the first time in a long while with her sisters, Carolyn and Erma, and her cousin Brenda. Her grandmother, Big Mama, now in a wheelchair, also attended the event.

The service began with a choir walking slowly into the darkened church, carrying candles and singing. Four thousand people had crowded into the church, cooling themselves with cardboard fans during the hot August evening. Prayers were led by her brother, Cecil. Reverend Jesse Jackson introduced the Franklin sisters, describing Aretha as "Sister Beloved, the one who wears the coat of many colors." Franklin performed solos, including two of her favorites, "Jesus Hears Every Prayer" and "Surely He Is Able." On other gospel classics, Franklin, her sisters, Mavis Staples, and the choir performed. The event even featured an altar call in which worshippers were invited forward to be baptized. Reverends Donald Parsons and Jaspar Williams, both admirers of C.L. Franklin, added powerful messages. The end result was an album that reflected the passion and might of the gospel sound and the excitement and energy of a revival meeting.

Following its 1987 release, *One Lord, One Faith, One Baptism* won two Grammys. One was for Aretha Franklin, for Best Soul Gospel Performance, Female. The other was for the Reverend Jesse Jackson, honoring his spoken-word contribution. "Gospel is and will always be an integral part of who I am," she wrote in her autobiography. "Gospel is all feeling and faith and about the life and teachings and miracles and trials and prophecies of Jesus, a music of unshakable conviction and determination that things will get better."

8

Hall of Fame

In 1987, Aretha Franklin became the first woman to be inducted into the Rock and Roll Hall of Fame. At the award ceremony, she was recognized as the "undisputed Queen of Soul" and as "a singer of great passion and control whose finest recordings define the term soul music in all its deep, expressive glory." Because of her fear of flying, Franklin did not attend the ceremony, but her fellow inductees that year were other performers she knew well, including Smokey Robinson and Marvin Gaye, as well as the two men who had shaped her career at Atlantic Records: Jerry Wexler and Ahmet Ertegun. Later, when a museum was built for the Rock and Roll Hall of Fame in Cleveland, Ohio, Franklin was able to travel to perform at the ceremony and see her display.

Through the Storm (1989) proved an appropriate title for Franklin's next album. On it, she again worked with Narada Michael Walden, and the album featured several duets, including "Gimme Your Love" with James Brown, "It Ain't Never Gonna Be" with Whitney Houston, "If Ever a Love There Was" with the Four Tops, and "Through the Storm" with Elton John. The title song received some popular airplay, but the album did not repeat the success of the albums that had preceded it.

At the time, Franklin was dealing with the difficult news that two of her siblings, Carolyn and Cecil, had both been struck with cancer. Carolyn's diagnosis came at a time when she was pursuing a college degree; she ultimately moved in with Aretha and soon required round-the-clock nursing care. She managed to achieve her dream of graduating, although she was by then too weak to attend the ceremony. Instead, Franklin hosted a graduation party at her home. Carolyn died on April 25, 1988, little more than a year after being diagnosed with cancer. Barely a year later, she lost her brother Cecil, also to cancer. The siblings' funerals were held at New Bethel Baptist.

The Best of Aretha Franklin

The Rock and Roll Hall of Fame has prepared a list of Aretha Franklin's "Essential Songs," the recordings that best represent the highlights of her career as a performer:

"Respect"
"I Never Loved a Man (The Way I Love You)"
"Chain of Fools"
"Baby, I Love You"
"Think"
"Rock Steady"
"(Sweet Sweet Baby) Since You Been Gone"
"Do Right Woman—Do Right Man"
"Spirit in the Dark"
"Amazing Grace"

Shortly thereafter, Franklin lost her grandmother, Big Mama, who had been living in a nursing home following an accident in which she fell out of bed and broke her hip. She died peacefully in 1990, yet it was another devastating loss for Franklin in a very short period.

HONORS AND AWARDS

In 1991, Franklin released *What You See Is What You Sweat*, which features a duet with Luther Vandross called "Doctor's Orders" and a remake of the Sly and the Family Stone classic "Everyday People." Her son Teddy played guitar on "You Can't Take Me for Granted," a song she wrote that apparently referenced a relationship in which she was involved at the time. The album also includes the French-influenced "What Did You Give" and "Ever Changing Times," featuring Michael McDonald on the chorus.

While the album was not as successful as earlier releases, Franklin continued to enjoy television appearances on such popular television programs as *The Arsenio Hall Show* and *Murphy Brown*. She also received numerous honors. In May 1992, she accepted a special Lifetime Achievement Award from the Rhythm & Blues Foundation. In 1993, she performed at two inaugural balls for President Bill Clinton, singing with such stars as Barbra Streisand, Fleetwood Mac, and Barry Manilow. Her song choice for the occasions, "I Dreamed a

DID YOU KNOW?

Aretha Franklin has recorded duets with a wide range of performers representing many different music genres. Over the years, her albums have featured performances with Frank Sinatra, John Legend, Mary J. Blige, Elton John, George Michael, Whitney Houston, Keith Richards, Ray Charles, Mavis Staples, Annie Lennox, Bonnie Raitt, Fantasia, Mariah Carey, Luther Vandross, Michael McDonald, and George Benson.

The recipients of the 1994 Kennedy Center Honors Awards attend a reception at the White House on December 4, 1994. From left to right are songwriter Pete Seeger, director Harold Prince, composer Morton Gould, singer Aretha Franklin, and actor Kirk Douglas.

Dream" from *Les Miserables*, included a reference to Martin Luther King Jr. and her ongoing support for his vision for the country. Because the president and his wife, Hillary, were fans of her music, Franklin performed for them on several occasions, including a performance in the White House's Rose Garden for the emperor and empress of Japan.

In 1994, Aretha Franklin became, at age 52, the youngest artist at the time to receive a Kennedy Center Honor. In its biography of Aretha Franklin, the Kennedy Center noted, "Her greatest achievement, perhaps, has been the ability to break down boundaries, to appeal to this country's vast range of musical tastes." Designed to recognize the lifelong achievements and accomplishments of the nation's "most prestigious artists," the Kennedy Center chose that year to honor Franklin as well as actor Kirk Douglas, composer Morton Gould, theater director and producer Harold Prince, and folk singer Pete Seeger. The honorees were invited first to the East Room of the White House for a special ceremony. Next, Franklin—wearing an elegant red dress—and the others were taken to the Kennedy Center, where they sat in the presidential box, enjoyed refreshments, and heard performances by artists such as Patti LaBelle, the Four Tops, and the choir from New Bethel Baptist Church.

That same year brought another major honor as well: Franklin was presented with a Lifetime Achievement Award from the Grammys. Her sons, Teddy and Eddie, were onstage with her when actor Danny Glover presented the award.

A DIVA

In 1998, Franklin released *A Rose Is Still a Rose*. Lauryn Hill wrote and produced the title song, and the result is a surprisingly contemporary sound from the 56-year-old singer. The song was a crossover hit, performing well on both the pop and R&B charts. The album itself went gold. As she noted in her autobiography, "To have an across-the-board hit at the end of the nineties, nearly forty years after my career began, is a source of tremendous satisfaction."

That same year, VH1 included Franklin in their *Divas Live* concert series, with Celine Dion, Gloria Estefan, Shania Twain, and Mariah Carey. The term *diva* comes from the Latin word for *goddess*. Traditionally, it has been used to refer to the principal female singer in an opera. More recently, it has come to be used as a description for a successful and glamorous female performer or celebrity. Franklin closed the concert with the powerful gospel song "Testimony." In 2001, VH1 dedicated its show to the work of Aretha Franklin, calling it *VH1 Divas Live: The One and Only Aretha Franklin*. Many leading singers turned out to honor the singer, including Marc Anthony,

Aretha Franklin onstage performing at *VH1 Divas Live: The One and Only Aretha Franklin* held at Radio City Music Hall in New York City, on April 10, 2001.

Nelly Furtado, Jill Scott, and Stevie Wonder. Franklin herself performed her classics "Chain of Fools" and "Think," as well as several gospel numbers.

One of her most amazing performances came a few years earlier, in 1998, at the fortieth annual Grammy Awards at Radio City Music Hall. A few nights earlier, Franklin had been asked to sing at a benefit for the charity MusiCares, where she had performed the aria *Nessun Dorma* from the opera *Turandot*. It had become the signature number for the great tenor Luciano Pavarotti, who attended the benefit and applauded Franklin's performance. Two days later, Franklin attended the Grammy Awards and sang "Respect." She then left the stage and went to her dressing room and prepared to leave. Suddenly, the producers of the telecast hurried into her dressing room. Pavarotti was scheduled to sing *Nessun Dorma* in 15 minutes, but he had become ill. Could Franklin sing in his place?

The performance was a demonstration of Franklin's true skill as an artist. With only minutes to prepare and no time to rehearse or to change the key of the arrangement to accommodate the difference between her range and Pavarotti's, Franklin walked onto the stage and the music began. The aria, arranged in a key to suit Pavarotti, began with Franklin singing in a far lower pitch than she normally sings, but the result was a rich sound that conveyed the emotion of the piece. The dramatic conclusion proved that she had mastered yet another genre of music—opera.

ARETHA TODAY

Today, Aretha Franklin continues to record, perform, and astound listeners. She continues to surround herself with contemporary artists to keep her music relevant to new generations of listeners. In 2007, she released *Jewels in the Crown: Duets with the Queen of Soul*, which paired her with such singers as Mary J. Blige, Fantasia Barrino, and John Legend. The duet with John Legend, "What Y'All Came to Do," is an upbeat, funky track that hearkens back to some of her classic recordings in the 1960s.

Legend wrote and produced the song. In the *New York Times*, he said of the recording session with Franklin, "She just goes in there and starts to experiment with the lyrics and the melody, and then creates her story, her interpretation of it. . . . She was so on target and so powerful and so precise."

For a while in the 2000s, Franklin's voice range seemed somewhat diminished, and she struggled to reach some of the higher notes she had once claimed with ease. But since giving up smoking and eliminating such things as soda, chocolate, and spicy foods from her diet, she has helped improve her vocal quality and range. Before a performance, she drinks hot tea and tries to keep silent for a half an hour or so.

Although she has accomplished so much in her career, Franklin's one unfulfilled wish is to study classical piano at the prestigious Juilliard School in New York. She was accepted into the program, but scheduling conflicts and other obligations have made it difficult for her to commit to the rigorous demands of full-time study. Instead, she arranges for classes when she is in the city.

While her fear of flying remains, she is hopeful that she will someday conquer it and once again see such places as Paris and the Middle East. "I am going to fly before it's all over again," she told the *New York Times*. "Even if it's just one more time." Although based in Detroit and prevented from traveling extensively, she continues to lend her support to many organizations and charities. Among these are the Joffrey Ballet, the National Alliance for Breast Cancer Organization, and the Detroit Symphony Orchestra. And she continues to write music and record new songs.

LEGACY OF THE QUEEN

The *New York Times* has described Aretha Franklin's voice as "one of the glories of American music. Lithe and sultry, assertive and caressing, knowing and luxuriant, her singing melts down any divisions between gospel, soul, jazz and rock, bringing an improvisatory spirit even to the most cut-and-dried pop material." *Rolling Stone* declared that Aretha Franklin is "not only the definitive female soul singer of the '60s, but one of the most influential and important voices in the history of popular music."

Franklin has made more than a dozen million-selling singles and has recorded 20 number-one R&B hits. She has proved her ability to perform in many different genres over the years, mastering gospel as a teenager, transitioning to standards and jazz, and then defining the sound of soul music in the 1960s. In more recent years, she has recorded successful pop and rock-influenced songs and has even wowed audiences when singing an opera aria.

In addition to her triumphs as a recording artist, Franklin has found success in other areas as well. She has formed a record label, World Class Records, based in her hometown of Detroit. Its mission is primarily to release gospel music and bring the sounds Aretha first sang as a girl to a new audience. In 1999, she published her autobiography, *Aretha: From These Roots*, and she has been exploring the possibility of making a movie based on this book.

In an article for *Rolling Stone* in 2004, as part of the selection of Aretha Franklin as one of its "greatest artists of all time," Jerry Wexler, who had helped shape Franklin's career in the 1960s, said:

> Genius is who she is, how everything is filtered through her consciousness. "Respect" had the biggest impact, truly global in its influence, with overtones for the civil rights movement and gender equality. It was an appeal for dignity. . . . No one could copy her. How could they? She's all alone in her greatness.

In their inclusion of Aretha Franklin in the "100 Most Important People of the Century," the editors of *Time* noted that she "helped bring spiritual passion into pop music." In "Respect," the magazine stated, Franklin made it clear that "women were no longer just going to stand around and sing about broken hearts; they were going to demand respect, and even spell it out for you if there was some part of that word you didn't understand." With such a powerful signature song, it is not hard to understand why so many female singers have pointed to Aretha Franklin as an inspiration or influence on their music and careers. Her power and passion can be heard in the voices of Chaka Khan, Mary J. Blige, her goddaughter Whitney Houston, and Mariah Carey.

Aretha Franklin's astonishing career, continuing now into her seventh decade, has proved that musical artists do not need to be limited to a single sound or single genre. Her impact on the music of the 1960s revolutionized expectations of female singers, and she provided an anthem for women and the civil rights movement. The pure joy of her early gospel recordings, the power of her soul songs, and the energy of her latest recordings provide evidence of the staying power of her career. By continuing to experiment with new sounds and new styles of music, she has made some missteps—not every album has been a hit—but has ensured that she will remain relevant as the recording industry evolves. Her voice remains unique, the sound of the "Queen of Soul."

1956   *The Gospel Soul of Aretha Franklin*

1961   *Aretha*

1962   *The Electrifying Aretha Franklin*; *The Tender, The Moving, The Swinging Aretha Franklin*

1963   *Laughing on the Outside*

1964   *Unforgettable: A Tribute to Dinah Washington*; *Runnin' Out of Fools*; *Songs of Faith*

1965   *Once in a Lifetime*; *Yeah!!! Aretha Franklin in Person* [live]

1967   *I Never Loved a Man the Way I Love You*; *Aretha Arrives*; *Take It Like You Give It*

1968   *Lady Soul*; *Aretha Now*; *Aretha in Paris* [live]

1969   *I Say a Little Prayer*; *Soul '69*

1970   *This Girl's in Love with You*; *Spirit in the Dark*

1971   *Young, Gifted and Black*

1972   *Amazing Grace* [live]

1973   *Hey Now Hey (The Other Side of the Sky)*

1974   *Let Me in Your Life*

1975   *You*

1976   *Sparkle*

1977   *Sweet Passion*

1978   *Almighty Fire*

1979   *La Diva*

1980   *Aretha*

1981   *Love All the Hurt Away*

1982   *Jump to It*

1983   *Get It Right*

1985   *Who's Zoomin' Who?*

1986   *Aretha*

1987   *One Lord, One Faith, One Baptism* [live]

1989   *Through the Storm*

1991   *What You See Is What You Sweat*

1997   *What a Difference a Day Makes*

1998   *A Rose Is Still a Rose*

2001   *Duets*

2003   *So Damn Happy*

2005   *Jazz Moods: 'Round Midnight*

2008   *This Christmas*

1942 Aretha Louise Franklin is born on March 25.

1946 The Franklin family moves to Detroit, where her father, C.L. Franklin, becomes pastor of New Bethel Baptist Church.

1956 She begins traveling and performing with her father's gospel revue. Her first album, *The Gospel Sound of Aretha Franklin*, is released.

1960 Franklin signs with Columbia Records.

1961 International Jazz Critics Poll names Aretha Franklin its New Female Vocal Star. She marries Ted White.

1966 She meets Jerry Wexler and signs with Atlantic Records.

1967 Franklin records songs for the album *I Never Loved a Man the Way I Love You*, including "Respect" and "Do Right Woman." *Billboard* magazine selects her as the top female singer of the year.

1968 February 16 is declared "Aretha Franklin Day" in Detroit. Chicago disc jockey Pervis Spann declares Franklin to be the "Queen of Soul." She appears on the cover of *Time*. Hits "Chain of Fools" and "Think" are released.

1971 She performs at the Fillmore West in San Francisco.

1972 Franklin records *Amazing Grace* over two nights at New Temple Missionary Baptist Church in Los Angeles.

1978 She marries actor Glynn Turman and signs a recording contract with Clive Davis at Arista Records.

1979 Franklin appears in *The Blues Brothers*. C.L. Franklin is shot by burglars in June; he will remain in a coma for five years.

1982 She returns to the top of the charts with *Jump to It*. She moves back to Detroit.

1983 Franklin begins to suffer from a fear of flying. She is no longer able to travel by plane to appearances.

1984   C.L. Franklin dies.

1985   *Who's Zoomin' Who?* is released. "Freeway of Love," a single from the album, becomes Franklin's first music video.

1987   Franklin becomes the first woman inducted into the Rock and Roll Hall of Fame.

1992   She receives the Lifetime Achievement Award from the Rhythm & Blues Foundation.

1993   Franklin performs at inaugural balls for President Bill Clinton.

1994   She becomes the youngest artist to receive a Kennedy Center Honor.

1998   Franklin appears in a *Divas Live* concert on VH1. With only a few minutes to prepare, she performs the opera aria *Nessun Dorma* in the place of ailing tenor Luciano Pavarotti at the Grammy Awards.

2001   VH1's 2001 *Divas Live* concert is dedicated to Aretha Franklin.

2007   *Jewels in the Crown: Duets with the Queen of Soul* is released, featuring Franklin performing with John Legend, Mary J. Blige, and Mariah Carey.

2009   Aretha Franklin sings at the inauguration of President Barack Obama.

Bego, Mark. *Aretha Franklin: The Queen of Soul.* Cambridge, Mass.: Da Capo Press, 2001.

Franklin, Aretha. *Aretha: From These Roots.* New York: Villard Books, 1999.

George, Nelson. *Where Did Our Love Go? The Rise and Fall of the Motown Sound.* Champaign, Ill.: University of Illinois Press, 2007.

Guralnick, Peter. *Sweet Soul Music: Rhythm and Blues and the Southern Dream of Freedom.* New York: First Back Bay, 1999.

Salvatore, Nick. *Singing in a Strange Land: C.L. Franklin, the Black Church, and the Transformation of America.* New York: Little, Brown & Co., 2005.

Wexler, Jerry. *Rhythm and the Blues: A Life in American Music.* New York: St. Martin's Press, 1994.

WEB SITES

American Masters: John Hammond
http://www.pbs.org/wnet/americanmasters/episodes/
john-hammond/about-john-hammond/626/

Aretha Franklin at All Music Guide
http://allmusic.com/cg/amg.dll

The Kennedy Center: Biography of Aretha Franklin
http://www.kennedy-center.org/calendar/index.cfm?fuseaction=
showindividual&entity_id=3729&source_type=A

The Rock and Roll Hall of Fame: Aretha Franklin
http://www.rockhall.com/inductee/aretha-franklin

page

3: PAT BENIC/UPI/Landov

9: Michael Ochs Archives/Getty Images

17: Michael Ochs Archives/Getty Images

25: Frank Driggs/Hulton Archive/Getty Images

29: SONY BMG MUSIC ENTERTAINMENT/Getty Images

34: Michael Ochs Archives/Getty Images

38: Michael Ochs Archives/Getty Images

44: Michael Ochs Archives/Getty Images

49: Michael Ochs Archive/Getty Images

53: © Roger Ressmeyer/CORBIS

56: Walter Bennett/Time & Life Pictures/Getty Images

67: Universal Pictures/Photofest

68: Jim Cooper/AP Images

74: Photofest

79: Doug Mills/AP Images

81: Scott Gries/ImageDirect/ Getty Images Entertainment/ Getty Images

Heather Lehr Wagner earned a B.A. in political science from Duke University and an M.A. in government from the College of William and Mary. She is the author of more than 40 books that explore social and political issues and focus on the lives of prominent Americans. She has contributed to biographies of Harriet Tubman, Sojourner Truth, Thurgood Marshall, Malcolm X, Frederick Douglass, Josephine Baker, and Martin Luther King Jr. in the BLACK AMERICANS OF ACHIEVEMENT, LEGACY EDITION series. She lives with her family in Pennsylvania.